the
GOOD GUT
DIET COOKBOOK
with prebiotics and probiotics

the
GOOD GUT
DIET COOKBOOK
with prebiotics and probiotics

Carolyn Humphries

LORENZ BOOKS

This edition is published by Lorenz Books, an imprint of Anness Publishing Ltd, 108 Great Russell Street, London WC1B 3NA; info@anness.com

www.lorenzbooks.com; www.annesspublishing.com; twitter: @Anness_Books

If you like the images in this book and would like to investigate using them for publishing, promotions or advertising, please visit our website www.practicalpictures.com for more information.

© Anness Publishing Ltd 2016

A CIP catalogue record for this book is available from the British Library.

Publisher: Joanna Lorenz
Project Editor: Joanne Rippin
Designer: Adelle Mahoney

PUBLISHER'S NOTE
Although the advice and information in this book are believed to be accurate and true at the time of going to press, neither the authors nor the publisher can accept any legal responsibility or liability for any errors or omissions that may have been made nor for any inaccuracies nor for any loss, harm or injury that comes about from following instructions or advice in this book. Both the author and publisher strongly recommend that a doctor or other healthcare professional is consulted before embarking on major dietary changes.

CONTENTS

INTRODUCTION

Our poor stomachs come under attack every day: many of us eat too much junk and processed foods; drink too much alcohol or fizzy sugary drinks or caffeine; and have way too much stress in our lives. We are subjected to pollution in the atmosphere every day and, generally speaking, we take too many antibiotic medications. These can lead to numerous conditions, from diarrhoea or constipation to more serious problems such as diverticulitis, type 2 diabetes, heart disease, colon cancer and obesity.

This book is not a wonder diet – instead it focuses on eating certain foodstuffs that really can help improve your digestion as part of a normal, healthy diet. In other words, it can help you to eat your way to feeling and looking a whole lot better.

If you consume the right foods, including those containing probiotics, prebiotics and fibre, and digest them properly, your whole body will function at its optimum. You'll be less sluggish as you will be detoxing naturally, getting rid of all the waste products efficiently – leaving your skin radiant, your hair shining, your nails strong and your tummy less bloated. It will also enable you to process and use what you eat properly so, unless you overeat, you should be able to reach and maintain the right weight for your height and build, slowly but surely. Another advantage to following this type of diet is that it can also help lower your cholesterol levels without the need for chemical intervention. So what have you got to lose?

Above: Summer berries are good sources of prebiotics.

Right: Matje herrings on pumpernickel bread, a double helping of probiotics.

Here you'll find everything you need to know about a healthy, balanced diet, including the all-important probiotics and prebiotics, which will help increase good bacteria in your gut. You'll find out how to incorporate them into a really enjoyable diet to help you set sail for a delicious voyage to a fitter, healthier you. The second part of the book is packed with tempting recipes, with an international feel to allow as much of a variety of ingredients and flavours as possible.

We've divided the recipes, for the most part, into those rich in probiotics and those high in prebiotics. Many have both properties (an added bonus), but by clearly labelling them, you can make sure that you get an excellent balance of each. Ideally, they need to work hand in hand for best results. So, after following our diet plan, try to make sure you still eat recipes from both sections or, at least, continue to eat some probiotics (see the tips for the best sources of probiotics on page 9) and some prebiotics (from the list on page 13) every day.

CAROLYN HUMPHRIES

BACTERIA MICROBES IN OUR GUT

We have about 100 trillion bacteria microbes in our guts – also known as our gut microbiota or gut flora. These microbes live and work throughout the digestive tract, with by far the largest concentration in the colon. If in the right balance, they help the body absorb food, assist in the production of B group vitamins (particularly B12) and vitamin K, play an important role in supporting our immune systems, and keep our digestive tract working properly and effectively.

There is a significant amount of research going on at the moment to determine the extent that these bacteria play on our health, but it is now widely believed that there are links between the balance of good (or 'friendly') bacteria and bad bacteria (germs) in our guts and many diseases, such as diabetes, colon cancer, ulcerative colitis and other

Eating more of the right foods and drinking plenty of water will improve your shape, health and well-being.

inflammatory conditions. They may also impact on obesity. Good bacteria is needed to fight off the bad in order to help prevent these illnesses.

There are about 1000 different types of bacteria in our guts. Everyone has different amounts of each, depending on their environment and their diet. People who eat a high carbohydrate diet have different gut flora from those who eat a high protein and fat diet, for instance. However, healthy people all have a similar balance of them and only relatively few types predominate. If you eat an unhealthy diet – with the addition of stress and the crazy, busy way we live our lives today in a polluted environment – the balance of bacteria is impaired, bad bacteria flourishes, and serious health issues can result.

Although you inherit your gut flora from your mother when you are born, the good news is that the balance of bacteria can be altered by making changes to your diet. This book will help you achieve this.

PROBIOTICS AND PREBIOTICS

PROBIOTICS

Probiotic bacteria have been consumed for thousands of years and have always been thought to promote good health. Some strains don't survive well in the gut, and there is no way of knowing exactly how many make it alive to your colon. It is thought that those that do make it (particularly bifidobacterium and lactobacillus) in a large enough quantity are able to multiply in the large intestine, changing the acidity and helping to prevent the growth of germs, or the harmful 'bad' bacteria (it's a simple case of good overcoming bad!). They can also help prevent and ease diarrhoea or chronic constipation, and some studies show that consuming probiotics regularly can alleviate symptoms such as abdominal pain, excessive flatulence, irregular and abnormal bowel motions, and bloating associated with Irritable Bowel Syndrome (IBS) and other similar illnesses.

Although more research is needed, there is evidence that the regular intake of probiotics in sufficient quantities may also boost the immune system, lower blood pressure and help reduce the symptoms of some allergies. There is no doubt that they do aid digestion and have a positive effect on a healthy gut.

Probiotic sauerkraut.

Fresh, homemade bio yogurt.

THE BEST SOURCES OF PROBIOTICS INCLUDE:
- some cheeses: bloom-rind cheeses (such as Camembert), blue cheeses and mature or sharp, hard cheese aged for more than 6 months, such as a good farmhouse Cheddar, Parmesan or mature Gouda, and brined cheeses, such as feta
- cultured milks such as bio yogurts, buttermilk, crème fraîche, smetana or sour cream, and kefir
- kimchi (an Asian side dish made from fermented Chinese (Napa) cabbage or other vegetables)
- Thai fish sauce (nam pla) and other fermented fish sauces from Asia
- pickles (naturally fermented ones, such as cucumbers, olives in brine, preserved lemons, and umeboshi plums)
- sauerkraut (fermented cabbage), see page 35
- sourdough breads
- soy products, including soya milk and naturally fermented (or brewed) soy and tamari (Japanese soy) sauces, miso (fermented soya paste), tofu (fermented soya bean curd), and tempeh (fermented soya bean 'cake')
- sprouted seeds and legumes
- vanilla pods (beans)

Check that soy and fish sauces are naturally fermented.

Natural fermentation

Good bacteria are produced when food naturally ferments – such as in yogurts, miso, sauerkraut and sourdough bread. Fermentation was first invented or discovered as a way of preserving foods long before we had refrigerators and freezers, but our ancestors soon discovered their health benefits.

Unfortunately, increasing naturally fermented foods in your diet is not as simple as popping to your supermarket and picking up a selection of foods. Many commercially made sauerkraut or pickles, for example, are often simply mixed with salt or vinegar and pasteurized for a long shelf life. This prevents the good (and bad!) bacteria from growing and is a far cry from properly brined and naturally fermented pickles. Some olives, for instance, are just treated to remove the bitterness and then packed in salt with sodium benzoate – a chemical preservative – then canned. That's not the same as fermenting them in brine for a decent length of time to preserve them, which, in turn, develops their wonderful flavour and allows the good bacteria to grow, resulting in

health benefits. Read the labels and check the ingredients for unwanted preservatives, such as sodium benzoate.

Although, obviously, you are unlikely to preserve your own olives, many traditional pickles, such as sauerkraut, are easy to make at home (see page 35). As a rule of thumb, the more tangy, salty and strong the pickle, the more likely it is to have plenty of good bacteria in it. Even natural vanilla extract contains additives – so you need to use vanilla pods (beans) and scrape the seeds yourself if you want health benefits, and not just the flavour.

Fermented sauces

Always read the label on your soy sauce, Thai fish sauce and other similar Asian sauces, to check they are naturally fermented (or it may say naturally brewed) without added colours, flavourings and unwanted chemicals. Also note they are high in salt so use sparingly (although some research shows that they may break down proteins into peptides that help inhibit the bad effects of salt on blood pressure, so that's another good reason to use them as a seasoning and dipping sauce).

Yogurt

Buying yogurt is also a bit of a minefield. Although all of them are good sources of calcium and are made with live cultures, some are better than others at supplying the good bacteria that you need. First and foremost, choose plain, natural yogurts, not sweetened ones. Secondly, look for live bio yogurt. It will have extra probiotic bacteria strains added to it (just read the labels, they will be clearly marked on it). They will best boost your gut flora. You can also try making your own (see page 42).

Probiotic hard cheeses

You need to be watchful about hard cheeses. Many so-called mature types are chemically 'aged' and not fermented or properly matured at all. A traditional farmhouse aged Cheddar, for instance, will be grainy and crumbly

Naturally aged Cheddar cheese has a grainy and crumbly texture that is similar to Parmesan.

(formed by lactic acid crystals) whereas a commercially 'aged' one may taste good and tangy but it will be close-textured and smooth. Go for artisan hard cheeses or ones that are clearly marked as having been matured for more than six months.

Soya milk

All soya (soy) milk has some probiotic properties but many commercial ones now have added cultures so they are the best ones to choose (the probiotics may also help the calcium to be absorbed easily).

Tofu

I used to dislike tofu as it seemed to be just a bland, strange-textured mass. However, now I've discovered how to utilize its wonderful silky properties and how to mix it with glorious flavours, which it absorbs readily,

I've changed my mind. For best results use firm tofu when you want chunks or slices and silken tofu when you are going to beat it up for a sauce or in a dessert or smoothie.

Pickled fish

Traditionally salted herrings, such as matjes, are great probiotics but, like most pickles, many pickled herrings in cans and jars are just the fish pickled in salt and vinegar with preservatives added, not traditionally preserved at all. I have found some matjes herrings in the supermarket but they're usually already in a sauce with a lot of additives. You can buy traditional ones all across Europe and the USA and from various online sources. You can also make your own (see page 37).

Quick-add probiotics

The good thing about probiotics is that you can add them to any meal without having to do anything to them. In fact they are best eaten uncooked (except for sourdough bread of course!) to get maximum benefits. So just think: 'Have probiotics with my meal'. For instance, serve some naturally fermented pickles or sauerkraut as a side dish with grilled fish or chicken. Add a good dollop of plain live

Left to right: firm tofu and matjes herring.

bio yogurt, crème fraîche or sour cream to garnish your soup or stew, or whizz one of them with fruit for a smoothie or into a dressing to drizzle on salad. Use tofu as a base for a creamy dip or, likewise, soy sauce makes a gorgeous dipping sauce with grated fresh ginger and some chopped spring onion (scallion) or is delicious added to salad dressings. Blend some blue cheese with herbs, oil and lemon juice and use as a salad dressing, stir some through a vegetable risotto, or blend it with crème fraîche to stir into pasta or cooked vegetables. Sprinkle your pasta or baked potato with grated Parmesan or aged Cheddar or have a small piece of one of these, or Camembert or Brie, with an apple for dessert or a snack. Crumble some feta over a salad or some spiced roasted vegetables.

Make sourdough bread centre stage – have a slice with your meal instead of potatoes, toast it for breakfast or make it into sandwiches for lunch. Having an aperitif? Go for naturally fermented pickled gherkins or olives or, perhaps, some kimchi as a nibble instead of your usual potato chips or salted roasted nuts.

PREBIOTICS
Prebiotics are a form of soluble fibre that pass through the gut undigested, stimulating the growth there of 'good' bacteria, such as species of lactococcus, bifidobacterium and lactobacillus. They also inhibit the growth of bad bacteria that produce toxins, such as Escherichia coli and Clostridia, thus helping to prevent serious gut disorders. All soluble and insoluble fibre is good for the digestive system but some foods contain specific prebiotic

Eat sourdough bread whenever possible.

substances called oligosaccharides, particularly inulin and oligofructose – both fructo-oligosaccharides – and lactulose and lactosucrose, which are lacto-oligosaccharides. Research has found that prebiotics have other health benefits. They may help the body absorb calcium (for healthy teeth and bones) and also boost the immune system. There are good indications, too, that they may help lower cholesterol levels in the blood, prevent some cancers and help relieve constipation and IBS.

Prebiotics are also added to some foods during their production. These include some yogurts, breakfast cereals, cereal bars and cheese products. It will be stated clearly on the labels where this is the case.

A note about barley: unprocessed barley is also thought to have prebiotic properties. I haven't included it in the list below as most of the time we eat processed pearl or pot barley.

Some breakfast cereals have prebiotics added to them.

THE BEST SOURCES OF PREBIOTICS INCLUDE:
- alliums such as leeks, garlic, spring onions (scallions) and onions
- asparagus
- bananas
- berries (strawberries, raspberries, blueberries etc.)
- broccoli (calabrese) and other cruciferous vegetables, such as cabbages
- celery
- cherries
- chicory (Belgian endive)
- dark (bittersweet) chocolate, minimum 70% cocoa solids (eat in moderation)
- honey (only eat in moderation)
- Jerusalem artichokes
- legumes (fresh and dried peas, beans and lentils)
- oats
- soya beans
- squashes
- tomatoes
- wheat

However, this is still an excellent addition to your diet as, even when polished, it is a great source of complex carbohydrates, and has plenty of soluble fibre and some insoluble fibre so it will help your gut. Eat in place of rice.

PLANT STANOLS AND STEROLS
Although these are not probiotics or prebiotics, they are plant-based substances present in small quantities in many of the same foods. They play an important role in digestion as they reduce the absorption of cholesterol from our gut into the bloodstream, allowing more of it to be excreted. This leads to a lowering of LDL (bad cholesterol) in the bloodstream without it affecting our HDL (good cholesterol). It can reduce the risk of furring up the arteries that lead to strokes and heart disease. Consuming these foods along with some dairy foods such as yogurt and cheese (so your probiotics can help here too) is the best way of getting the cholesterol-lowering effects of the stanols and sterols. Some yogurt drinks and margarine-type spreads are fortified with plant stanols and sterols, and can help reduce blood cholesterol.

THE PROCESS OF DIGESTION

Just having an understanding of how your body digests its food (even in this simplified description) may help you to see how important it is to put the right foods into your mouth. Just a thought to bear in mind: if you eat more food for energy (calories) than your body needs, it doesn't just excrete it all, it is taken into the body and stored as fat to be used later, but if you don't exercise it carries on being stored.

1 Before you even take your first bite, the thought, look and smell of your food gets your gastric juices flowing. First your mouth waters as saliva gets ready to begin the breakdown of the food once you pop it in your mouth and signals are sent to your brain to alert your stomach that food is on its way.

2 As you start to chew the food, grinding and mashing it with your teeth and tongue, it mixes with saliva. Your tongue also picks up the taste,

The digestive process begins before you start eating.

Drink plenty of water during the day, and with meals.

sending more signals to your brain to get more gastric juices flowing in your stomach. The saliva starts the breakdown of complex carbohydrates (starch) into glucose. As you swallow the food, it moves down the oesophagus into the stomach, mixing with more saliva. Drinking water during your meal will also help the digestive process.

3 The stomach muscles contract, mashing the food into a pulp, called chyme, with gastric juices – a mixture of enzymes and hydrochloric acid. The chyme is then pushed along past the liver, to be mixed with bile from the pancreas, which helps break down fats ready to be absorbed into the bloodstream. The pancreas also excretes enzymes, which break down the proteins into amino acids and complete the process of breaking down starch into glucose.

4 The processed food then moves into the small intestine. Here it is hit with more chemicals to break down the nutrients into absorbable molecules and a mass of bacteria that help too. The wall of the small intestine is lined with thousands of fronds, called villi, filled with tiny blood vessels and these absorb many of the nutrients into the bloodstream to be used by the body.

5 Any undigested food, including the fibre, is moved through to the colon (a part of the large intestine), which is teeming with even more bacteria. If there are plenty of prebiotics in the food, they will aid good bacteria growth. The good bacteria get to work breaking down

Vegetables and fruit are rich in fibre to aid digestion.

GUT DISORDERS

As you've seen above, probiotics and prebiotics, along with plenty of fibre and water, can help enormously in getting the gut flora in the right balance for optimum digestion. By gradually increasing your probiotics, prebiotics and fibre, you can help prevent IBS, diverticulitis, ulcerative colitis, constipation and other digestive disorders.

Consumption of probiotics may also help shorten a bout of gastroenteritis and can help sufferers of chronic constipation. Eating/drinking them regularly may also help reduce the symptoms of IBS. However, if you already have IBS, some prebiotic foods may actually be trigger foods for you. The only way of knowing is by keeping a food diary. If you find specific foods – such as tomatoes – make your symptoms worse, then, of course, they need to be avoided. That doesn't mean that all prebiotics will have the same effect so you should still be able to build up your good gut flora by consuming those ones that don't cause a problem. You may also find that cooked fruit and vegetables rather than raw cause less problems too.

tough fibres, enzymes and the last of the proteins into amino acids. The soluble fibre forms a gel to soften the stools and bind cholesterol to the faeces. In a healthy gut, the colon absorbs the excess water and the muscles squeeze the waste products, including the fibre, into a stool. The stool is then excreted through the rectum. If the balance of bacteria is wrong, toxins and inflammation develop, causing a range of bowel disorders, including diarrhoea. If there isn't enough water or fibre, constipation arises, making the stools hard and difficult to pass, and also encouraging the growth of bad bacteria and a build-up of toxins, which can, in turn, lead to serious health problems.

BALANCING YOUR DIET

Eating well and wisely is something we should all aspire to. It doesn't mean slaving for hours over a hot stove every day; it means choosing good, simple fresh ingredients and putting them together in the right proportions to give us a nutritious and enjoyable diet. Many of the probitic and prebiotic recipes you are going to see later in the book will incorporate plenty of these ingredients but they are not designed to be eaten to the exclusion of other foods in the groups listed on the following pages. You'll see from the eating plan on pages 29–31 how to combine them easily into delicious, healthy meals and snacks. There is cooking involved of course (this is a recipe book after all) but, there are plenty of simple minimum-effort ideas too.

Complex carbohydrates

These are starchy carbs found in cereals, rice, pasta, pulses, starchy tubers such as potatoes and yams, bread and crackers. It's the starches that give a mealy texture – a good clue that the food you are eating contains them. The starch is broken down into glucose in the body to give us energy. Wholegrains, such as brown rice, oats and wholemeal (whole-wheat) flour are better than the highly processed white versions, as they contain all the fibre and nutrients we need and, because they contain all the fibre, take longer to be processed in the body, helping to keep our blood sugar levels constant and our gut working properly. That doesn't mean you can never have a bowl of white pasta or a pearly white risotto ever again, but it's a good idea to have the brown ones most of the time. White flour is often fortified with calcium, iron and B vitamins that are lost in the refining so it's not all bad.

Changing from white to wholemeal pasta is an easy transition and a good tip, to start with, is to cook it a little longer than instructed so it is softer, or you may find it a bit 'chewy' at first. If that is just too much, look for the white ones with added fibre – they are a good halfway stage. When eating potatoes, try to cook them with their skins on (and eat the skins). Not only do you get all the fibre but a lot of the other nutrients they contain are just under the skin. Of course, sometimes only white, fluffy mash will do – and that's fine, just make sure you get plenty of fibre from other foods in the meal, such as from other vegetables or fruit with their skins on, some pulses or legumes, or, maybe, some nuts or seeds. We should eat plenty of complex carbohydrates such as these every day.

Left to right: oatcakes, wholewheat spaghetti and a baked potato, all excellent sources of fibre.

Vulnerable groups, such as pre-school children, people who have been ill and the elderly should not eat too many wholegrain foods because, if the appetite is very small or impaired, the bulk from the fibre can fill them up too quickly and mean they don't eat enough other nutrients. So for these groups, fortified white bread and similar is better (or, at most, half and half with wholegrains).

Simple carbohydrates

These are all the sugars that we consume: the natural fructose found in honey, fruit and vegetables; lactose, found in milk; and sucrose – the table sugar we add in its many forms: white, brown, molasses, golden (corn) syrup and so on. There is huge confusion about sugar. It has become a dirty word but you have to understand the difference. Natural sugars found in fruit, vegetables and milk are good ways to give us masses of essential nutrients and some fast energy. They also make dishes taste naturally sweet and pleasant. Honey, too, contains some nutrients and antioxidant properties, and is now shown to be a prebiotic – so good for our gut – and should be the added sweetener of choice (although in small quantities). Sucrose – and all the other commercial sugars and syrups, and I include agave syrup in this category – are all processed sugars which just add empty calories

Natural sugars from fruit are beneficial to the gut.

to our food and can cause not only tooth decay but obesity, diabetes and heart disease. They are unnecessary and should be avoided as much as possible or, at least, kept to a minimum.

Cutting down on high added sugar in your diet is one of the best ways to improve your health. Of course, you can still enjoy the occasional piece of cake or a biscuit but, if you do, try to have them as a special treat and choose ones that, at least, contain other healthy ingredients, such as oats or wholemeal flour, plenty of nuts and seeds, and/or dried fruit. If buying any ready-made ones, check the labels and buy the ones with the lowest added sugar content. It's difficult to go by the nutrition label as any sugar measurement will include the natural sugar in other ingredients in the food, such as the dried fruit or milk. Better to look at the ingredients list. If sugar or a sugar derivative is listed, make sure it is well down at the bottom (or, ideally, not there at all!). All ingredients are listed in order of quantity so if sugar is the first ingredient or even near the top, leave it well alone! The way forward is to use just a little honey when you need to cook with sugar, or to add extra sweetness, and avoid added processed sugars as much as possible.

Proteins

These are vital for growth, maintenance and repair. They can be divided into two groups: complete (mostly animal) proteins and incomplete (plant) proteins. They are made up of a number of amino acids. All meat, poultry, fish, eggs and dairy products are complete proteins, so contain all eight essential amino acids our body needs and cannot make itself. Three speciality grains are also complete proteins – quinoa, amaranth and buckwheat – so they are great options for vegetarian meals. All other plant proteins, found in pulses and legumes, soya products, nuts and seeds (and some in wholegrains) are incomplete proteins because they do not contain all eight essential amino acids. Each plant protein contains a different mix of amino acids so it is important, if you are vegetarian, to eat a good variety – especially if you are vegan and don't eat dairy products or eggs. There are 12 other non-essential amino acids in foods that our body can make itself so the body will only take these from our food if, for some reason, it cannot make enough.

You only need a small amount of protein at each meal, though, and make sure any meat you eat is lean.

Dairy produce

Milk, yogurt, cheese, cream, buttermilk, sour cream and crème fraîche all provide us with the most easily absorbed calcium, vital for the growth of healthy teeth and bones. They also give us protein, vitamin A, some B vitamins and other essential vitamins, minerals and fat. Three portions of dairy-type products a day are recommended. If you can't tolerate cow's milk products, you may be able to eat sheep's or goat's milk ones. There are non-dairy choices, such as soya, oat and nut milks, and various non-dairy cheeses, creams and yogurts. The only drawback is that, although they are sometimes fortified with calcium, it isn't as easily absorbed so you need to get more calcium from tofu, fortified bread, fresh or canned fish (eat the soft bones!), nuts, broccoli and other dark greens. Guidelines still recommend going for semi-skimmed (low-fat) milk and opting for low-fat cheeses and yogurts. There is huge debate on whether the added carbs in lower fat products do more harm than the fat itself but, particularly if you are watching your weight or in a risk group for heart disease or strokes, it makes sense to have lower-fat options.

A note about creams: they are high in saturated fat so it is not good to have too much. It's better to go for crème fraîche or sour cream (reduced fat options are again a matter of choice) as, at least, they have probiotic properties that are going to help your gut.

A rainbow of fruit and vegetables

We should eat as many different fruit and vegetables as we can every day. Not only are they packed with essential vitamins and minerals, they also give us the vital gut fibre we need. They're packed with carotenoids and flavonoids, which have great antioxidant properties to boost our immune systems. The different colours have different properties, which is why it's so important to eat dark leafy greens and beans, bright red, orange and yellow tomatoes, (bell) peppers, berries, carrots and squashes, right through to deep purple beetroot (beets) and blueberries.

Dairy products contain calcium and some are probiotic.

The importance of fibre

There are two forms of fibre in our food – soluble and insoluble (as already discussed, pre-biotics are a form of soluble fibre). Both are vital for keeping our gut – and heart – healthy.

Soluble fibre is found mainly in fruit, vegetables, pulses, wholegrains (that is unprocessed grains), nuts and seeds. It is called soluble because it dissolves in water in our gut and forms a gel. This slows the absorption of glucose into the bloodstream and so stops little surges of sugar when we've just eaten, keeping our energy levels on an even keel. Soluble fibre also helps keep our stools soft so preventing constipation. Its third role is to bind cholesterol to the faeces for excretion so less of it is absorbed into the bloodstream, therefore lowering blood cholesterol levels and so helping prevent heart disease.

Insoluble fibre is the sort we probably all think of as fibre, which used to be called roughage. It doesn't dissolve – hence its name – and it can be found in the fibrous

husks of grains, seeds and pulses and the skin and membranes of fruit and vegetables. Insoluble fibre isn't broken down in the digestive process at all; it passes through the gut, with the help of water, helping to move other foods with it to pass through the digestive system more easily, so preventing constipation and other gut-related problems.

Barley is an excellent source of soluble fibre.

Scrub, rather than peel, root vegetables when possible.

Fats

All fats play an important role in our diets even though some have a bad reputation. We need them to help our brains function properly, and they are necessary for cell formation, to help keep us warm and to regulate body temperature. They also keep the skin supple and can be used for energy. They're vital for the absorption of the fat-soluble vitamins A, D, E and K, too. The body uses what it needs but any excess fats are stored as body fat so it's important not to eat too much.

There are four main types of fat. The first group is saturated fats, found mainly in meat, poultry and dairy produce. This sort of fat, if eaten in excess, may lead to furred-up arteries and high blood cholesterol levels. That's why it's important to choose lean meat, cut off fat and skin and, for some people, to go for lower-fat dairy alternatives. Coconut oil is also high in saturated fat but unrefined coconut oil is considered beneficial to health.

Polyunsaturated fats (in fish and vegetable oils) are a good bet. They contain omega 3 fatty acids, to help brain function, and for healthy eyes and blood, and have been linked to helping prevent heart disease. They're primarily found in fish oils (particularly oily fish such as salmon, mackerel, herring, sardines, and trout and in fresh, not canned, tuna) and also in linseeds, pumpkin seeds, sunflower seeds, rapeseeds, soya and walnuts and their oils, though they're not so easily processed by the body. Polyunsaturated fats also contain omega 6 fatty acids, for growth and boosting the immune system, and are found in avocados, nuts, seeds, eggs and plant oils.

The third group is monounsaturated fats, also found in avocados and plant oils, including olive, nuts and seeds and their oils. They are known to help reduce 'bad' LDL cholesterol in the blood. The fourth group is hydrogenized fats. These are plant fats that have been processed and behave like saturated fats. They are found in some processed foods and should be avoided as they raise bad LDL cholesterol levels and reduce good HDL cholesterol levels. The less refined the oils you choose the better, so go for cold-pressed extra virgin and avoid over-processed non-specific 'vegetable' oils.

A note about butter: many people prefer butter on bread for its flavour, and this is better than generous amounts of margarine (though you may prefer to use a plant sterol and stanol one to help lower your cholesterol). Likewise for some cooking, only butter will do. The key is to use all fats sparingly. But for a change, try dipping lovely, fresh sourdough bread in extra-virgin olive or rapeseed oil instead of spreading with butter during a meal – simply delicious!

Water – the essential fluid

Vital for life, water makes up about 60 per cent of the body so without it we'd dehydrate and shrivel up. But it's also vital for us to function

Left to right: lean red meat, salmon and olive oil, three healthier ways of incorporating fat into your diet.

properly. Not only does it keep our brain and every cell in our body working, without it we'd overheat because we wouldn't sweat and we couldn't even blink as we wouldn't have any tears to lubricate our eyes! But one of its other key roles is to assist our digestion.

Water helps food pass through the body and aids its absorption. It also facilitates the easy excretion of waste products at the end of the digestive process, so helps prevent constipation, and helps flush out toxins. If you drink plenty you are also less likely to get urinary tract infections, kidney stones and colon cancer. It's so important that we drink at least 6–8 glasses a day and more when the temperature rises or when doing aerobic exercise. It doesn't have to be pure water (though this is ideal) – all drinks count but some are better than others. You should avoid those with added sugars, such as squashes and fizzy drinks and go easy on pure fruit juices (best limit them to drinking as part of a meal unless well-diluted with still or sparkling water, because they still contains a lot of sugar, albeit natural fructose, that coats the teeth and can cause tooth decay). It is better to eat whole fruit for the most part as they include the fibre that you need. Coffee and tea also count in your daily fluids but watch your intake of caffeine. Too much acts as a diuretic, leaching your body of water, and it can impair the absorption of calcium. It is interesting to note that if you feel thirsty, you are already dehydrated, so keep the fluid levels topped up all day. One of the commonest causes of headache is dehydration so try sipping water and see if the pain goes. A good indicator that you aren't drinking enough is the colour of your urine. It should be very pale. The darker the colour, the more you need to drink.

If plain water is not your preference, try filling a jug with water and adding some slices of citrus fruit or cucumber, or mint leaves (see carminatives below) and chill in the refrigerator to sip as you fancy it during the day. Freshly-grated ginger or cinnamon sticks infused in boiling water and flavoured with a little honey are also particularly good as they not only taste great, but aid digestion too. Other drinks such as herbal or fruit teas or rooibos (redbush), which is caffeine-free, are also good, and one of the best ways to start the day is to sip a mug of boiling water with a slice of lemon added (sweetened with a tiny spoonful of honey if need be).

Alcohol

Alcoholic drinks are, of course, fluid but they also act as a diuretic, so will dehydrate you rapidly. Many alcohols such as wine, beer and cider are fermented so are, arguably, better for you than spirits BUT you should limit your intake to recommended guidelines, usually around 2–3 units a day for women and 3–4 units a day for a man, with two or three alcohol-free days a week. Using alcohol in cooking is fine because the alcohol is driven off by boiling (but not if you add it into a cold dessert like a trifle!).

CARMINATIVES

Some herbs and spices are carminative (an agent that relieves flatulence) and are really good for aiding digestion, so include them when you can. Ones with particular benefits are:

• basil	• coriander seed	• galangal	• parsley
• caraway	• cumin	• ginger	• sage
• cardamom	• dill	• mint	• star anise
• cinnamon	• fennel (herb and	• mustard	• thyme
• cloves	seed)	• nutmeg	• turmeric

RAW FOOD VERSUS COOKED

Some foods are best eaten raw to get their full benefits but others are more beneficial broken down by cooking to make their nutrients more readily available for absorption into our bodies.

PROBIOTICS AND PREBIOTICS

All probiotics are better eaten raw for maximum benefits as many of the bacteria will be destroyed by temperatures over about 58°C/ 136°F, so, basically, when cooked for any length of time. Dairy-based ones, such as yogurt, crème fraîche or sour cream should, when possible, be stirred in at the end of cooking (this is essential if you use low-fat options anyway as they will split if cooked at a high temperature!). Olives and pickles, too, are best added at the end, when you can, or eaten as a garnish or side dish. Obviously sourdough bread has to be cooked but by this time the bacteria has already formed lactic acid to promote good bacteria growth and it makes all the nutrients much easier to digest. Even if you use white flour, the lactic acid reduces the

Cooked or raw, eat as many vegetables as possible.

bread's GI (Glycaemic Index), too, so white sourdough bread doesn't raise blood sugar levels like ordinary white bread. Obviously, sometimes you want to eat long-fermented probiotics, such as sauerkraut, soy sauce, tofu and cheese in cooked dishes, which is fine so long as you eat them raw most of the time, because, although the good bacteria will mostly be destroyed, the foods become what are known as 'metabiotic' and will aid the growth of good bacteria in your gut even if they don't add to them directly. Prebiotic grains, chocolate and honey can be eaten raw or cooked as heat doesn't affect oligosaccharides.

FRUIT AND VEGETABLES

It is important to eat a range of vegetables and fruit – not just prebiotic ones but all of them – every day, cooked and raw, but it is interesting to know the benefits of eating them either way, and the best way of cooking them.

Vitamins are affected by heat. B vitamins and vitamin C are water-soluble, so leach into cooking water. That's why it is important to incorporate the vegetable cooking water into a dish when possible. Never use more water than absolutely necessary for cooking, although steaming is preferable as the minimum nutrients will be lost. Vitamins A, D, E and K are fat-soluble so will leach into oil but won't be affected by water. Deep-frying is not recommended anyway as a healthy way of cooking; it is much better to stir-fry very quickly in just a little oil as fewer nutrients are lost and the oil is then also eaten with the food, so any vitamins that have been absorbed by the oil will also be consumed.

You may be surprised to discover it is preferable to eat broccoli raw (along with other cruciferous vegetables) or just very quickly and briefly cooked as the enzymes, known as glucosinates, are damaged by high heat thus reducing some of their health-giving properties. Remember, however, if eating raw, it's important to cut them up small so they can be chewed and digested more easily. Always prepare your fruit and veg just before use whenever possible because nutrients are lost when surfaces are exposed to the air by chopping or slicing.

Likewise, because vitamin C is the most easily destroyed by heat, you'll get the maximum benefit if you eat those foods richest in it raw, such as citrus fruit, berries, kiwi fruit, peppers and so on. But that doesn't mean you should never eat them cooked because other benefits they provide may be better obtained that way. Take tomatoes, for instance. They're rich in vitamin C so, yes, are good eaten raw, but if slowly cooked they release more antioxidant properties, which can guard against infections and free-radicals (unstable molecules made by oxygen in our bodies that attack the DNA and then attach themselves to healthy cells, damaging them, which may cause heart disease and some cancers and suppress the immune system). The same goes for asparagus and many other fruit and vegetables.

Frozen fruit and vegetables are a very healthy alternative to fresh because they are processed so soon after harvesting, so they lose very few nutrients. Freezing doesn't damage them and they can be cooked quickly too.

Frozen peas are as nutritious as fresh ones.

Cooking tomatoes releases more antioxidants.

MAINTAINING A HEALTHY GUT

Once you've understood the basic principles of probiotic and prebiotic foods, you should find it easy to give your digestive system the help it needs to maintain a healthy balance of the right bacteria.

A gradual change is best

You could experience flatulence, bloating and diarrhoea if you increase your intake of probiotics, prebiotics and fibre too quickly. The symptoms will disappear as your body adjusts but they can be avoided if you start gradually. If you are used to all-white bread, rice and pasta, start by just having some wholegrains interspersed with your usual white ones (either half and half, or some meals wholegrain and some meals white), then increase the wholegrains and decrease the white.

Some people will experience no symptoms at all – and if you are already eating wholegrains and a good amount of live bio yogurt, fruit and vegetables, you will be fairly well adjusted to this style of eating – so can just incorporate more into the daily routine for great results quickly. I just want to emphasize, convert little by little and enjoy them as part of a mixed, healthy diet and your body will thank you for it.

Eat more, from left to right: oats, nuts and lentils.

EAT PLENTY OF THESE FOODS:
- All wholegrains: wholemeal (whole-wheat) or buckwheat pasta and bread; brown rice; spelt and rye bread; barley (pearl barley still contains a lot of fibre and nutrients even though its husk has been removed); and oats and other grain cereals, such as quinoa, bulgur wheat and millet.
- Fish: oily fish, such as salmon, mackerel or sardines; white fish, such as pollock and cod; and shellfish (or for vegetarian alternatives with omega 3 fatty acids: soya products, nuts and seeds).
- All fruit and vegetables (fresh or frozen).
- Pulses and legumes.
- Nuts, seeds and dried fruits.
- Some chicken and other poultry (without skin) and/or vegetarian alternatives such as eggs and soya products.
- Some dairy products: milk, yogurt, cheeses (particularly the probiotic ones).

Detox and weight loss

When you eat an unhealthy diet, packed with fat and sugar and low in fibre, your body just can't cope with it and you end up with all the unpleasant side-effects: bloating, flatulence, constipation, abdominal pain, lethargy and bad

GO EASY ON OR AVOID THESE FOODS:
- Cakes, biscuits, cookies, sweets, candy and sugary drinks: make smoothies instead.
- Commercially processed and cured meats, such as ham, bacon and sausages.
- Red meat: a few small portions of lean meat a week is fine as it is rich in protein, vitamins and minerals. Fatty meats, such as belly pork, lamb breast or brisket of beef, unless very well-trimmed, are best avoided or only eaten occasionally.
- Too much processed white flour, such as supermarket white sliced bread (if you have to choose it, better to go for one with added fibre or a multiseed variety).
- Ready-meals and takeaways should be eaten very occasionally. They are notoriously high in fat, salt and sugar.
- Salty snacks, such as roasted salted peanuts and fried crisps (US potato chips): choose raw nuts or dried fruit instead.
- Deep-fried foods: go for grilled, broiled, baked, steamed or stir-fried instead.

Keeping active will help you achieve a healthy weight.

skin. The reason being that all the bad bacteria feeds on that waste food lurking in your colon, creating toxins, which, in turn 'poison' your body and make you feel lousy. When you eat plenty of probiotics, prebiotics and fibre, and drink plenty of water, as part of a good, balanced diet, the food passes through your gut slowly, the nutrients are processed efficiently and all the waste products are excreted in a comfortable, timely manner, leaving your body feeling as good as it can.

If you are already overweight, changing to this type of diet will stimulate your gut to work properly and ensure that you are eating a much healthier diet in the right proportions so you should find that you lose weight gradually and effectively. It isn't a miracle cure, it is a healthy and sensible long-term strategy. Plus, because

Make smoothies instead of buying sugar-filled drinks.

everything is working so efficiently, providing you keep active, with several bursts a week of aerobic exercise that gets your heart pumping, such as swimming, running, active sport, strenuous housework or gardening, you should be able to maintain a healthier weight.

EATING A GUT-FRIENDLY DIET

Hopefully, after reading the introduction to this book, you will realise that tweaking an already healthy diet to include more prebiotic and probiotic foods is actually fairly easy. On the next few pages there are some quick and easy ways to add good bacteria to your gut to use alongside the recipes that follow.

The following meal ideas are designed primarily for people who already eat a well-balanced diet. Obviously mix and match meals as you like, bearing in mind, colour, flavour and texture – you wouldn't want poached eggs on wholemeal toast for breakfast, egg sourdough sandwiches with tomatoes for lunch and an egg-based quiche for dinner, for instance. Variety is the key. If you prefer to have your main meal at lunchtime then just swap a lunch for a dinner and so on. This is just a guide so you can see how easy it is to get into the way of making sure you get a healthy diet with plenty of the prebiotics and probiotics incorporated. In reality, if you make a banana bread, for instance, you will have a slice most

Always wash fruit and vegetables before eating.

FOOD HYGIENE
Basic cleanliness while preparing food and sensible cooking and storage are also essential for your health so please bear the following in mind.
- Wash your hands before preparing food.
- Wash and dry fresh produce before use.
- Don't taste food and stir it with the same spoon.
- Use different chopping boards for fruit and vegetables, meat, poultry and fish.
- Use different cloths to wipe down a chopping board you have been using for cutting up meat, and work surfaces.
- Don't put raw and cooked meat on the same shelf in the refrigerator.
- Store leftovers in a clean container covered with a lid in the refrigerator. Don't put warm food in the refrigerator.
- When reheating food always make sure it is piping hot throughout.
- Don't re-freeze raw foods that have defrosted unless you cook them first.

afternoons or mid morning for your snack until it's used up, not have different bakes each day, and you probably won't choose to eat all the selected recipes either.

Here are a few ideas for quick and easy lunches and dinners. Most are ideas for one person but you can cook or prepare as much as you need for a family. Some dinner suggestions use cans or packs that are enough for two to three people (and it's stated in the suggestion). Simply double up or, if you are cooking for one, freeze in portions for future use. Finish off your meal with fresh fruit and/or live yogurt.

Lunch ideas
- Hummus with wholemeal (whole-wheat) pitta bread, tomatoes and celery sticks.
- Sourdough or wholemeal bread, bloom-rinded, blue or aged hard cheese, tomatoes and pickles (preferably naturally fermented ones of course!).
- Tuna, egg or chicken salad with a live bio yogurt dressing; include some prebiotic vegetables, such as onion, tomato, celery and chicory (Belgian endive) in the salad.
- Baked potato topped with grated aged cheddar, or sour cream and coleslaw.
- Sachet of miso soup (simply add to a bowl and pour in boiling water), with a few very thinly sliced spring onions (scallions) and a sprinkling of sesame seeds on top.
- Oatcakes with nut butter and plenty of cherry tomatoes and celery.

NOTES ON THE RECIPES
Ingredients are given in imperial, metric and American measures. Follow one set only. American terms are given in brackets. The ingredients are listed in the order in which they are used in the recipe.

Spoon measures are level unless otherwise stated. Eggs are medium (US large) unless otherwise stated. Individual vegetables or fruits are average-sized unless otherwise stated. A handful is the amount you can hold comfortably in the palm of your hand. Always wash, peel (unless otherwise stated), core and seed fresh produce, if necessary, before use.

All can and packet sizes are approximate as they vary from brand to brand. For example, if we list a 400g/14oz large can of tomatoes and yours is a 397g can that's fine. Choose cans of fruit or vegetables in natural juice or water and no added sugar or salt.

Given cooking times are approximate and should be used as a guide only. Always check the food is piping hot and cooked through before serving.

Always preheat the oven and cook on the shelf just above the centre unless otherwise stated (fan ovens may not need preheating and the positioning of the food is less crucial).

Left to right: hummus, tuna salad, and miso soup sprinkled with spring onions and sesame seeds.

Dinner ideas

- Tofu cubes marinated in soy sauce, grated ginger and sesame seeds, grilled or broiled on skewers with (bell) peppers. Serve with brown rice tossed in soy sauce and lemon.
- Grill a steak and serve with sautéed onions, grilled tomatoes, green beans and a baked potato topped with a spoonful of sour cream and some chopped chives.
- Smear basil pesto over a chicken breast and grill. Serve with brown rice and a mixed salad (including prebiotic vegetables).
- Lightly steam some mangetout (snow peas), carrot sticks, spring onions (scallions) cut in short lengths and shredded pak choi (bok choy) for a few minutes only. Place in a bowl of miso soup (make up a sachet with boiling water), add some cooked buckwheat noodles and top with either some diced tofu or a grilled salmon steak, flavoured with naturally fermented soy sauce.
- Simmer pearl (pot) barley in chicken or vegetable stock (1 part barley to 3 parts stock) until tender with cubes of butternut squash and some chopped spring onions thrown in. Crumble in some blue cheese and season to taste. Serve with a mixed salad including prebiotic vegetables.
- Cook wholemeal (whole-wheat) pasta and add small broccoli florets for the last 3 minutes' cooking time. Drain, return to the pan and stir in smoked salmon strips and a spoonful of cream fraîche seasoned with a dash of Thai fish sauce and black pepper.
- Simmer a can of chopped tomatoes, 15ml/ 1 tbsp tomato purée (paste), and 2 or 3 chopped spring onions until pulpy. Stir in a small handful of chopped fresh basil and a drained can of tuna. Season. Mix with cooked wholewheat spaghetti, and serve topped with a scattering of capers and some grated Parmesan cheese, with a green salad, including courgettes (zucchini), chopped celery and spring onions.

Left: tofu and pepper kebabs with fresh ginger and sesame seeds. Right: wholemeal spaghetti with a tuna and tomato sauce.

14-DAY EATING PLAN

The following table contains a more defined two-week plan of how to structure each day to follow a diet that is high in prebiotics, probiotics and fibre. It is a good idea to commit to at least two weeks, and see if at the end of this period you feel that your digestion has improved and symptoms such as bloating, excessive wind and general discomfort have been relieved. Once that has been achieved, you can be less strict and simply get into the habit of adding in pre- and probiotics on a daily basis.

DAY 1

BREAKFAST	Glass of pure fruit juice • Porridge with sliced banana and a drizzle of honey
Mid-morning snack	Zesty Soya Smoothie (see page 147)
LUNCH	Watercress, Pear and Roquefort Salad (see page 79) • An apple and a handful of raisins or a couple of dates
Mid-afternoon snack	Slice of Wholemeal Sunflower Bread (see page 142), lightly buttered
DINNER	Grilled pork chop with Potato, Onion and Garlic Gratin (see page 115), carrots and green beans and a spoonful of Sauerkraut (see page 35) • Berries with yogurt

DAY 2

BREAKFAST	Glass of pure fruit juice • Poached egg and wilted spinach on sourdough toast
Mid-morning snack	Banana
LUNCH	Leek and Oatmeal Soup (see page 52) with a slice of sourdough bread, small wedge of aged Cheddar cheese, tomatoes, celery and pickled cucumber • Bunch of grapes
Mid-afternoon snack	Fruity Muesli Bar (see page 133)
DINNER	Beef Stew with Star Anise (see page 96) • 2 satsumas

DAY 3

BREAKFAST	Glass of pure fruit juice • Sugar-free muesli (granola) topped with plain live bio yogurt and a handful of blueberries
Mid-morning snack	Pear
LUNCH	Coleslaw with Blue Cheese (see page 81) on a baked potato • A few pieces of dried mango
Mid-afternoon snack	Honey and Almond Cookie (see page 132)
DINNER	Chicken Tagine with Olives and Lemon (see page 90) • Chocolate Sorbet with Red Fruits (see page 126)

DAY 4

BREAKFAST	Mango and Lime Lassi (see page 146)
Mid-morning snack	Oatcake with a scraping of butter and yeast extract, or peanut butter
LUNCH	Salt Herring Open Sandwiches (see page 70) • Banana
Mid-afternoon snack	Apple and 2 squares 70% cocoa solids chocolate
DINNER	Duck and Broccoli Stir-fry (see page 94) • Little Blueberry Pie (see page 122)

DAY 5

BREAKFAST	Glass of tomato juice • Porridge with chopped nuts and seeds, sliced strawberries and a drizzle of honey
Mid-morning snack	Small wedge of Camembert and a stick of celery
LUNCH	Potato Curry with Yogurt (see page 101) • Cherry tomatoes and cucumber • 3 plums
Mid-afternoon snack	Wholemeal Scone (see page 141)
DINNER	Butter Bean Stew (see page 103) with a slice of sourdough or wholemeal (whole-wheat) bread and a green salad • Date and Tofu Ice (see page 129)

DAY 6

BREAKFAST	Zesty Soya Smoothie (see page 147)
Mid-morning snack	Small sandwich made with 1 thin slice of sourdough bread with a scraping of butter, a sliced tomato and ground black pepper
LUNCH	Grilled Leek and Courgette Salad (see page 74) with a few oatcakes or wholemeal (whole-wheat) crackers • Plain live bio yogurt with a handful of raisins
Mid-afternoon snack	Slice of Banana Bread (see page 134)
DINNER	Lamb Kebabs with Salsa (see page 98) with warmed flat bread • Fresh mango slices, topped with a dollop of crème fraîche, some chopped pistachio nuts, grated fresh ginger and a drizzle of honey

DAY 7

BREAKFAST	Glass of pure fruit juice • Scrambled eggs on wholemeal toast with grilled (broiled) tomatoes and mushrooms
Mid-morning snack	Nectarine
LUNCH	Blue Cheese and Leek Soup (see page 53)
Mid-afternoon snack	Oatcake with a scraping of butter and honey
DINNER	Sautéed turkey escalope with lemon, capers and new potatoes • Sauerkraut Salad with Cranberries (see page 118) • Strawberry Mousse (see page 127)

DAY 8

BREAKFAST	Cranberry Juice (see page 152) • Plain live bio yogurt with a sprinkling of rolled oats, and a handful of mixed, dried fruit and chopped nuts
Mid-morning snack	Oatcake spread with Hummus (see page 66)
LUNCH	Chunky Tomato Soup with Noodles (see page 57) • Slice of melon with a sprinkling of ground ginger
Mid-afternoon snack	Orange and Avocado Juice (see page 149)
DINNER	Roast chicken breast with Catalan-style Roasted Vegetables (see page 114) • Tofu Berry Cheesecake (see page 124)

DAY 9

BREAKFAST	Strawberry and Tofu Smoothie (see page 148)
Mid-morning snack	Thin slice of Wholemeal Sunflower Bread (see page 142) with a scraping of peanut butter
LUNCH	Blue Cheese and Leek Soup (see page 53) • 3 plums
Mid-afternoon snack	Banana
DINNER	Salmon with Whipped Yogurt Sauce (see page 87) • Mixed roast vegetables • A crisp salad or Classic Cabbage Kimchi (see page 40) • Fruit salad of melon, raspberries and blueberries topped with chopped dates

DAY 10

BREAKFAST	Glass of Red Defender (see page 151) • Grilled mushrooms on wholemeal toast
Mid-morning snack	Broccoli Booster (see page 155) and a few cashew nuts
LUNCH	Salad Rolls with Pumpkin and Tofu (see page 72) • Banana
Mid-afternoon snack	Fruity Muesli Bar (see page 133)
DINNER	Pollock with Onions (see page 85) • Steamed baby potatoes and Savoy cabbage • Blueberry Honey Ice Cream Parfait (see page 130)

DAY 11

BREAKFAST	Glass of pure fruit juice • Sugar-free muesli soaked in apple juice topped with a dollop of plain live bio yogurt, chopped apple and blackberries
Mid-morning snack	Finger-sized wedge of creamy, ripe Brie spread in some chicory (Belgian endive) spears
LUNCH	Garlic and Butternut Squash Soup (see page 54) • A slice of sourdough bread with a scraping of butter, if preferred • Fresh peach
Mid-afternoon snack	Wholemeal Scone (see page 141) topped with crème fraîche, a drizzle of honey and a few fresh blueberries.
DINNER	Chiang Mai Dip with Steamed Vegetables (see page 67) • Stir-fry of chicken, cooked brown rice, peas, a dash of soy sauce and Chinese five-spice powder • Pineapple

DAY 12

BREAKFAST	Glass of pure fruit juice • Omelette with snipped chives • Slice of sourdough toast and a scraping of butter
Mid-morning snack	Oatcake spread with Olive Tapenade (see page 65)
LUNCH	Cheese and Yogurt Dip (page 64) with a wholemeal flat bread and crudités • Banana
Mid-afternoon snack	Pear and 2 squares of 70% cocoa solids chocolate
DINNER	Tofu and Green Bean Red Curry (see page 100) served with noodles • Plain live bio yogurt with orange segments and strawberries and a drizzle of honey

DAY 13

BREAKFAST	Half a grapefruit • Porridge with chopped apple and cinnamon stirred in and drizzled with honey
Mid-morning snack	Glass of Basil Blush (see page 156)
LUNCH	Brie and Black Olive Tart (see page 102) with green salad • A handful of cherries
Mid-afternoon snack	Small, thin wholemeal honey sandwich with a sprinkling of chopped walnuts
DINNER	Thai Prawn Salad with Frizzled Shallots (page 88) • Strawberries with crème fraîche and a couple of squares of melted 70% cocoa solids chocolate drizzled on top

DAY 14

BREAKFAST	Fresh orange and grapefruit segments • Boiled egg with wholemeal toast with a scraping of butter, and yeast extract, if liked
Mid-morning snack	Oatcake with a little Hummus (see page 66)
LUNCH	Gravadlax with Horseradish (see page 68) with pumperkickel • 3 fresh apricots
Mid-afternoon snack	Handful of raw nuts and raisins
DINNER	Chicken with 40 Cloves of Garlic (see page 91) • Steamed broad (fava) beans and spring onions (scallions) • New potatoes in their skins, sprinkled with chopped parsley • Coffee Bananas (see page 128)

MAKING PROBIOTICS

As discussed in the introduction, many commercially made pickles, and some sourdough breads in particular, are not really probiotic as they haven't been allowed to ferment naturally in the traditional way. The ideal solution to this is to make your own, which is not difficult at all. Apart from pickles, you can also make your own yogurt (below), sauerkraut (left) and fresh, crisp sprouted seeds, peas and beans.

MAKING PICKLES AT HOME

The two most important things to remember when making pickles at home is firstly to use ingredients that are as fresh as possible and secondly that any utensils and jars or bowls are scrupulously clean before use – as you would do if you were making any type of preserves.

Rinse bowls, knives, boards etc in boiling water and leave to drain, and immerse muslin, cheesecloth or rubber sealer rings and metal lids in a bowl of boiling water and leave until required. Follow the tips below to sterilize your jars and bottles for storing everything, from yogurt to sauerkraut. That way you will ensure that your foods stay as fresh as possible, and you can enjoy the fruits of your labours for longer.

Store the unopened jars in a cool, dark place, and once opened keep in the refrigerator and use within two weeks.

Metal-clasped storage jars are completely airtight and can be sterilized over and over again.

Sterilizing

To sterilize your storage jars or bottles, use one of the four following methods:
- Place jars or bottles in the microwave (not suitable for metal clasp jars), add 60ml/

Use the freshest ingredients possible when pickling or preserving any food.

4 tbsp water to each and microwave for 2–3 minutes until the water boils. Drain (use oven gloves to pick up the jars) and place upside down on kitchen paper to dry.
- Put the clean jars, bottles and lids in a pan of water on the hob. Cover, bring to the boil and switch off the heat. Leave until required.
- Put clean jars, bottles, and lids in a cool oven at 140°C/275°F/Gas 1 for 15 minutes.
- Put jars, bottles and lids upside down in the dishwasher and run through a hot wash.

SAUERKRAUT

Sauerkraut has a sharp, pungent flavour that goes very well with meats and cheeses. The most nutritious way of serving it is cold as a salad or just warm as a side dish, which is how we've used it in this book but the plus is that, even if cooked, it can still help production of good microbes in the gut.

1.2kg/2½lb white cabbage, core removed, finely shredded
25g/1oz coarse kosher or sea salt
7.5ml/1½ tsp spices such as caraway, crushed juniper berries and black peppercorns

Makes about 1.2kg/2½lb

NUTRITIONAL INFORMATION Energy 324kcal/1356kJ; Protein 16.8g; Carbohydrate 60g, of which sugars 58.8g; Fat 2.4g, of which saturates 0g; Cholesterol 0mg; Calcium 590mg; Fibre 33.6g; Sodium 9909mg

1 Toss the shredded cabbage with the salt and spices. Leave to stand for 10 minutes, then rub with the hands until the cabbage is limp. Pack into a large sterilized crock or bowl with a lid.

2 Weigh down the cabbage with a plate that fits inside the crock or bowl. Cover loosely with a lid or large plate and cover with a clean dish towel to prevent dust (or bugs!) getting in. Leave in a cool place (below 20°C/70°F) for 1 week.

3 Remove the lid or plate and skim off any scum with a spoon. Repeat daily until no more scum appears, about 1–4 weeks. This means that the cabbage is ready. Transfer into sterilized jars, seal and store in the refrigerator for up to 1 month.

DILL PICKLES

Classic cucumber pickles are enjoyed with everything from cheese to burgers. They are delicious sliced and added to salads and are great for an easy probiotic addition to many meat, poultry or fish dishes. Some people even snack on them straight from the jar.

20 small, ridged or knobbly
  pickling (small) cucumbers
2 litres/3½ pints/8 cups water
90g/3½oz/½ cup coarse sea salt
15–20 garlic cloves, unpeeled
2 bunches fresh dill
15ml/1 tbsp dill seeds
30ml/2 tbsp mixed pickling spice
1 or 2 hot fresh chillies

Makes about 900g/2lb

NUTRITIONAL INFORMATION Energy 76kcal/305kJ; Protein 5.3g; Carbohydrate 11.4g, of which sugars 10.7g; Fat 0.8g, of which saturates 0g; Cholesterol 0mg; Calcium 140mg; Fibre 4.6g; Sodium 10013mg

1 Scrub the cucumbers in cold water. Leave to dry. Put the measured water and salt in a large pan and bring to the boil. Turn off the heat and leave to cool until at room temperature.

2 Using the flat side of a knife blade or a wooden mallet, lightly crush each garlic clove, breaking the papery skin.

3 Pack the cucumbers tightly into one or two wide-necked, sterilized jars, layering them with the garlic, fresh dill, dill seeds and pickling spice. Add one chilli to each jar.

4 Pour the cooled brine into the jars, making sure that the cucumbers are completely covered. Tap the jars on the work surface to dispel any trapped air bubbles.

5 Cover the jars with lids and then leave to stand at room temperature for 4–7 days before use. Store in the refrigerator.

SALT HERRINGS

This is a simple version of making your own salt herrings, which although not as well fermented as traditional matjes herring will still give you good health benefits. It is vital that your fish is very fresh and everything is scrupulously clean to make this dish.

600g/1lb 6oz very fresh herring
    fillets, skinned
2 shallots, thinly sliced
15ml/1 tbsp sea salt
2.5ml/½ tsp black peppercorns
5ml/1 tsp clear honey
1 bay leaf
bottled, still mineral water or
    cooled, boiled water
rye bread, thinly sliced red onion
    and sprigs of fresh dill, to serve

**Makes one 1 litre/1¾ pint/
4 cup jar**

NUTRITIONAL INFORMATION Energy 76kcal/305kJ; Protein 5.3g; Carbohydrate 11.4g, of which sugars 10.7g; Fat 0.8g, of which saturates 0g; Cholesterol 0mg; Calcium 140mg; Fibre 4.6g; Sodium 10013mg

1 Feel the fish all over and remove any fine bones with tweezers (called pin-boning). Cut the fish in 2.5cm/1in chunks.

2 Place the fish in a bowl, previously rinsed in boiling water. Add the shallots, salt, peppercorns and honey. Toss until everything is well combined.

3 Pack the fish into a sterilized 1 litre/1¾ pint/4 cup preserving jar, pressing it down well. Add the bay leaf. Add pure bottled water (or cooled boiled water) to cover the fish by at least 2cm/¾in. Seal and chill in the refrigerator for 48 hours.

4 When ready to eat, taste the fish. If too salty rinse and pat dry. Serve on rye bread with thinly sliced red onion and dill.

UMEBOSHI

These traditional pickled plums are a speciality of Japan, where they are often eaten for breakfast with rice. They are highly prized for their probiotic qualities and go beautifully in many recipes from fish to duck, or can be eaten with some aged Cheddar or creamy Camembert and oatcakes or wholegrain crackers for a delicious snack.

1kg/2¼lb ume (Japanese plums) or apricots, washed and soaked overnight in cold water
60ml/4 tbsp shochu or white wine
190g/6½oz coarse sea salt

Makes about 1kg/2¼lb

NUTRITIONAL INFORMATION Energy 350kcal/1505kJ; Protein 9.1g; Carbohydrate 72.4g, of which sugars 72.4g; Fat 1g, of which saturates 0g; Cholesterol 0mg; Calcium 170mg; Fibre 22.7g; Sodium 58972mg

1 Drain the plums and remove the stem. Pat dry with a clean cloth, place in a large freezer bag and sprinkle 45ml/3 tbsp shochu or white wine evenly over the fruit. Add 150g/5oz of the salt to the bag, and shake so it is evenly distributed.

2 Put 20g/¾oz salt in a deep non-metallic bowl, then transfer all the fruit to the bowl and evenly sprinkle the fruit with the remaining salt. Sprinkle with 15ml/1 tbsp shochu or white wine.

3 Place a plate that will fit in the bowl on top of the fruits and put a 4–5kg/9–11lb weight on top. Seal the bowl with clear film or plastic wrap, cover tightly with a cloth and leave to cool.

4 Place in a cool place away from direct sunlight for about 10 days or until the liquid rises above the level of the plate. Put a lighter weight (about 2–2.5kg/4½–5½lb) on top of the fruits and leave wrapped for another 10–15 days. Drain.

5 Spread the salted fruits on a flat bamboo strainer or a rack (so air can circulate) and air-dry (preferably in sunlight) for 3 days. Store in clean screw-topped jars in a cool, dark place.

PRESERVED LEMONS

These richly flavoured fruits are widely used in Middle Eastern cooking. Usually whole lemons are preserved, but this recipe uses wedges, which can be packed into jars more easily. Often added to recipes at the beginning of cooking – and sometimes they need to be – but you will get maxium probiotic benefit if you add them after cooking.

10 unwaxed lemons
sea salt
200ml/7fl oz/scant 1 cup lemon
   juice

**Makes two 1.2 litre/2 pint/
5 cup jars**

NUTRITIONAL INFORMATION Energy 128kcal/536kJ; Protein 6.6g; Carbohydrate 22.4g, of which sugars 22.4g; Fat 1.8g, of which saturates 0.6g; Cholesterol 0mg; Calcium 529mg; Fibre 0.3g; Sodium 19682mg

1 Wash the lemons well and cut each into six to eight wedges. Press a generous amount of sea salt on to the cut surface of each wedge.

2 Pack the salted lemon wedges into the warmed, sterilized jars. To each jar add 30–45ml/2–3 tbsp sea salt and about 100ml/3½fl oz/scant ½ cup lemon juice, then top up with boiling water to cover the lemon wedges. Seal the jars and leave to stand for 2–4 weeks before using.

3 To use, rinse the preserved lemons well to remove some of the salty flavour, then pull off and discard the flesh (unless your recipes calls for the whole fruit to be used). Cut the lemon rind into strips or leave in chunks and use as required. The salty, well-flavoured juice in the jars can be used to flavour salad dressings or added to hot sauces.

CLASSIC CABBAGE KIMCHI

This is an elegant kimchi, which you can cut into bite-sized chunks as and when you want to eat it. It will keep in the refrigerator for several months and the flavour will get stronger with age as the cabbage ferments more and so produces more 'good' bacteria.

1 large head (or 2 small) Chinese
   leaves (Chinese cabbage), about
   2kg/4½lb
30ml/2 tbsp fine sea salt
50g/2oz/¼ cup coarse sea salt
75ml/5 tbsp water

For the seasoning
½ Chinese white radish,
   about 500g/1¼lb, peeled
   and thinly sliced
25g/1oz chives
25g/1oz watercress or rocket
   (arugula)
5 garlic cloves
15g/½oz fresh root ginger, peeled
½ onion
½ Asian pear, or ½ kiwi fruit
   (optional)
3 spring onions (scallions), sliced
50g/2oz/¼ cup Korean chilli
   powder, or dried red chilli flakes
120ml/4fl oz/½ cup Thai fish sauce
5ml/1 tsp mild clear honey
1 red chilli, sliced

Serves 10–12

NUTRITIONAL INFORMATION Energy 107kcal/446kJ; Protein 4.3g; Carbohydrate 13.8g, of which sugars 13.1g; Fat 4g, of which saturates 0.3g; Cholesterol 0mg; Calcium 122mg; Fibre 5.2g; Sodium 384mg

1 Make a deep cut across the base of the head of the Chinese leaves and split the head in two. Repeat this with the two halves, splitting them into quarters. Then place the quartered head in a bowl and cover it with water, adding the 30ml/2 tbsp fine salt. Leave the quarters to soak for around 2 hours.

2 Drain the cabbage and sprinkle with the 50g/2oz/¼ cup coarse sea salt, making sure to coat between the leaves, then sprinkle over the water. Leave to stand for 4 hours.

3 Cut the radish slices into fine strips. Cut the chives and watercress or rocket into 5cm/2in lengths. Finely chop the garlic, ginger, onion and the Asian pear or kiwi fruit, if using. Combine in a bowl with all the other seasoning ingredients, together with 120ml/4fl oz/½ cup cold water.

4 Rinse the softened quarters of Chinese leaves in cold running water. Place in a large sterilized container with a sealable lid and coat with the seasoning mixture, ensuring that the mixture gets between the leaves and that no leaf is left uncovered. The outermost leaf of each quarter of cabbage will have softened. This can be wrapped tightly around the other leaves to help the seasoning permeate throughout the whole.

5 Cover loosely with the lid and then a clean dish towel to prevent dust or anything else getting in. Leave to stand at room temperature for 5 hours, then seal the lid and leave in the refrigerator for at least 24 hours before eating.

COOK'S TIP
For a simpler dish, cut the Chinese cabbage into rough chunks before soaking and then drain and mix with all the flavourings before covering and leaving to mature as above.

LIVE YOGURT

It is easy and economical to make yogurt at home – simply make sure that you use live bio yogurt as a starter and that it is as fresh as possible. Once you have made the first batch, you can reserve some of the yogurt as a starter for the next.

600ml/1 pint/2½ cups full-fat (whole), semi-skimmed (low-fat) or skimmed milk
15–30ml/1–2 tbsp live bio yogurt

Makes about 600ml/1 pint/ 2½ cups

NUTRITIONAL INFORMATION Energy 404kcal/1680kJ; Protein 20.5g; Carbohydrate 28.1g, of which sugars 28.1g; Fat 23.5g, of which saturates 15.2g; Cholesterol 84mg; Calcium 732mg; Fibre 0g; Sodium 267mg

1 Pour the milk into a pan and bring to the boil. Remove the pan from the heat and leave the milk to cool to 45°C/113°F. Ideally use a thermometer for best results but if you don't have one, test with a clean finger – the milk should feel slightly hotter than is comfortable. Pour the milk into a medium sterilized bowl.

2 Whisk in the yogurt – this acts as a starter. Leave in the bowl or transfer it to a large jar. Cover with clear film or plastic wrap, then insulate the bowl or jar with several layers of dish towels and leave in a warm place. Alternatively, transfer the milk to a vacuum flask to keep it warm.

3 Leave for 10–12 hours until thickened. Transfer to a sterilized, sealable container and store in the refrigerator.

SPROUTED SEEDS, PULSES AND GRAINS PROBIOTIC

Larger pulses, such as chickpeas, take longer to sprout than small beans such as mung or soya, and seeds such as mustard and cress, but they are all easy to grow and are usually ready to eat in three or four days. Eat them as fresh as possible.

45ml/3 tbsp mung or soya beans, mustard or cress seeds

Serves 4

NUTRITIONAL INFORMATION Energy 42kcal/175kJ; Protein 4.1g; Carbohydrate 1.8g, of which sugars 0.6g; Fat 2.1g, of which saturates 0.3g; Cholesterol 0mg; Calcium 27mg; Fibre 2.4g; Sodium 1mg

1 Wash the beans or seeds thoroughly in water, then place them in a large, clean jar. Fill the jar with lukewarm water, cover with a piece of muslin or cheesecloth – or a new disposable kitchen cloth – and fasten securely with a rubber band. Leave in a warm place to stand overnight.

2 The next day, pour off the water through the muslin and refill the jar with water. Shake gently, then turn the jar upside down and drain thoroughly. Leave the jar on its side in a warm place, away from direct sunlight, preferably 13–21°C/55–70°F.

3 Rinse thoroughly 3 times a day until the sprouts reach the desired size (4–5 days). Remove the sprouts from the jar, rinse, and discard any ungerminated ones. Store the sprouts in a covered container in the refrigerator for up to 3 days.

SOUPS

Not just a wonderful way to get plenty of fruit and vegetables into your diet, soups are also full of loads of probiotics and prebiotics. Add a hunk of freshly baked sourdough or wholemeal bread for the perfect accompaniment! Many are substantial enough for a meal, others would be delicious followed by more of the same bread or oatcakes and some bloom-rinded cheese or aged hard cheese such as Cheddar, some celery and juicy tomatoes and, perhaps, even a pickled cucumber or two.

CUCUMBER SOUP WITH SALMON

The refreshing flavours of cucumber in this soup fuse with the hint of heat in the salsa and charred salmon to bring the taste of summer to the table. This recipe gives a good hit of probiotics from the yogurt and crème fraîche, and omega 3s too from the salmon.

3 medium cucumbers
300ml/½ pint/1¼ cups live bio
    Greek (US strained plain) yogurt
250ml/8fl oz/1 cup vegetable
    stock, chilled
120ml/4fl oz/½ cup crème fraîche
15ml/1 tbsp chopped fresh chervil
15ml/1 tbsp snipped fresh chives
15ml/1 tbsp chopped fresh parsley
1 small red chilli, seeded and very
    finely chopped
a little sunflower oil, for brushing
225g/8oz salmon fillet, skinned
    and cut into eight thin slices
salt and ground black pepper

Serves 4

NUTRITIONAL INFORMATION PREBIOTIC Energy 208kcal/869kJ; Protein 12.6g; Carbohydrate 12g, of which sugars 1.7g; Fat 12.5g, of which saturates 5.5g; Cholesterol 52mg; Calcium 89mg; Fibre 1.1g; Sodium 420mg

1 Peel two cucumbers and halve lengthways. Scoop out and discard the seeds, then roughly chop the flesh. Purée in a food processor or blender, then add the yogurt, stock, crème fraîche, chervil, chives and seasoning, and process until smooth. Chill.

2 For the salsa, peel, halve and seed the remaining cucumber. Cut the flesh into small neat dice. Mix with the chopped parsley and chilli. Chill until required.

3 Brush a frying pan with oil and heat until very hot. Sear the salmon slices for 1–2 minutes on each side, until slightly charred. Ladle the chilled soup into bowls. Top each with two slices of salmon and a spoonful of salsa and serve.

BUTTERMILK, HONEY AND ALMOND SOUP

PROBIOTIC

This is based on a traditional Danish recipe where sweet soups are often served for dessert. It's light and frothy, with subtle sweetness and lemony notes. The buttermilk gives a nutritious, probiotic, creamy richness.

2 large eggs, separated
1.5ml/¼ tsp cream of tartar
60ml/4 tbsp orange blossom
   honey, or other flowery, but not
   too strong honey
1 vanilla pod (bean), seeds scraped
2.5ml/½ tsp grated lemon zest
1.5 litres/2½ pints/6 cups
   buttermilk
50g/2oz/¼ cup flaked (sliced)
   almonds, toasted, to decorate

Serves 6

COOK'S TIP
Raw eggs are not
recommended for very
young children, the infirm
and pregnant women.

NUTRITIONAL INFORMATION PROBIOTIC Energy 241kcal/1017kJ; Protein 12.5g; Carbohydrate 34.2g, of which sugars 34g; Fat 7.3g, of which saturates 1.2g; Cholesterol 73mg; Calcium 346mg; Fibre 0.6g; Sodium 136mg

1 Whisk the egg whites until frothy in a medium bowl then add the cream of tartar. Continue whisking until stiff peaks form. Set aside.

2 In a second bowl, beat the egg yolks with the honey. Add the vanilla seeds and lemon zest. Stir in the buttermilk and blend the mixture thoroughly.

3 Gently fold the egg whites into the buttermilk mixture, until completely blended. Serve immediately in soup plates or bowls, decorated with the toasted, flaked almonds.

CREAMY CUCUMBER AND TOMATO SOUP

PROBIOTIC

This soup comes from Russia and is based on their much-loved smetana, a type of sour cream. Crème fraîche can be used instead. Easy to make and lovely for a light lunch on a lazy summer day, it is packed with probiotics and some prebiotics and makes the perfect, healthy choice. You can use Dijon mustard but I find the flavour slightly sharp so you may need to increase the amount of honey slightly.

2 eggs
15ml/1 tbsp mild German or
American mustard
100ml/3½fl oz/scant ½ cup
smetana or crème fraîche
1 litre/1¾ pints/4 cups buttermilk
(or half buttermilk half
ordinary milk)
2–3 firm tomatoes, skinned,
seeded and diced
1 cucumber, total weight 250g/9oz,
very finely sliced
1 bunch spring onions (scallions),
finely sliced
5–10ml/1–2 tsp mild clear honey
45ml/3 tbsp finely chopped
fresh dill
sea salt and white pepper
a little cold milk, to thin

Serves 6

NUTRITIONAL INFORMATION Energy 353kcal/1473kJ; Protein 27.6g; Carbohydrate 17.6g, of which sugars 17.3g; Fat 19.8g, of which saturates 10.3g; Cholesterol 169mg; Calcium 363mg; Fibre 0.8g; Sodium 305mg

1 Put the eggs in a pan, cover with cold water and bring to the boil. Reduce the heat and simmer for 10 minutes. Drain and put under cold running water. Shell the eggs and separate the yolks from the whites. Reserve the whites.

2 Put the egg yolks in a soup tureen or bowl and mash until smooth. Add the mustard and the smetana or crème fraîche and mix together.

3 Slowly add the buttermilk or buttermilk and milk mixture to the egg yolk and smetana mixture, and blend. Gradually add a little cold milk to thin to the desired consistency, if necessary.

4 Finely chop the reserved egg whites and add to the bowl together with the diced tomato and sliced cucumber and spring onions. Finally stir in the honey and chopped dill and season with salt and pepper to taste.

5 Chill in the refrigerator for 30 minutes to allow the flavour to develop. To serve, ladle the soup into soup bowls.

FRESH-TASTING ASPARAGUS SOUP

PREBIOTIC

This soup is a great blend of prebiotics and probiotics and is a good way to use the first thin cuttings of asparagus, if available, in which case reduce the cooking time to 2 minutes.

2 carrots, chopped
1 parsnip, chopped
3 celery sticks, chopped
1 large onion, chopped
2 bay leaves
450g/1lb fresh asparagus, trimmed
    and cut into 2.5cm/1in pieces
25g/1oz/2 tbsp butter
35g/1¼oz/generous ¼ cup spelt
    flour
250ml/8fl oz/1 cup crème fraîche
1 egg yolk
salt and ground white pepper

Serves 4

NUTRITIONAL INFORMATION Energy 353kcal/1457kJ; Protein 6.1g;
Carbohydrate 11g, of which sugars 4.2g; Fat 31.8g, of which saturates 19.3g;
Cholesterol 130mg; Calcium 88mg; Fibre 2.2g; Sodium 76mg

1 Bring 1.5 litres/2½ pints/6 cups water to the boil in a large pan and add the carrots, parsnip, celery, onion and bay leaves. Cook, uncovered, over a medium heat for 15–20 minutes, until tender. Strain through a sieve or strainer. Discard the vegetables.

2 Meanwhile, in a separate pan, cook the asparagus in 250ml/ 8fl oz/1 cup water over a medium-high heat for 3–4 minutes. Drain the cooking water into the reserved vegetable stock, and refresh the asparagus under cold water.

3 Melt the butter in a clean pan over a medium heat, and stir in the flour. Cook for 2 minutes, stirring, then slowly stir in stock. Bring to the boil, stirring, and simmer for 2 minutes. Remove from the heat and stir in the egg yolk. Add the asparagus and stir in the crème fraîche, reheat, season to taste, and serve.

GREEN BEAN AND CABBAGE SOUP
PREBIOTIC

Summer savory is an aromatic, pungent herb that has a natural affinity with all kinds of beans; sage is a good substitute. This recipe is packed with prebiotic cabbage.

500g/1¼lb floury potatoes, peeled
    and cut into pieces
2 onions, chopped
300g/11oz Savoy cabbage, cut into
    quarters, core removed, and
    sliced into 2.5cm/1in pieces
300g/11oz green beans, cut into
    1cm/½in lengths
1 small bunch of fresh summer
    savory or sage, chopped
50ml/2fl oz/¼ cup olive oil
sea salt

Serves 4

NUTRITIONAL INFORMATION Energy 239kcal/998kJ; Protein 6.2g; Carbohydrate 34.2g, of which sugars 11.7g; Fat 9.6g, of which saturates 1.4g; Cholesterol 0mg; Calcium 96mg; Fibre 6.1g; Sodium 20mg

1 Put the potatoes and onions in a large pan, add 1 litre/ 1¾ pints/4 cups water and bring to the boil. Cover and simmer for about 20 minutes, until tender.

2 Transfer the potatoes, onions and cooking liquid to a food processor or blender and process to a purée. Return to the pan.

3 Add the cabbage, beans and savory or sage to the pan and cook over a medium heat for a few minutes, until the cabbage is cooked, and the beans are just tender but still with some bite. Season with salt to taste, stir in the olive oil and serve.

LEEK AND OATMEAL SOUP

Both leeks and oatmeal are great prebiotics and go together really well in this simple, nutritious soup. Serve with some grated aged Cheddar on top if you wish.

600ml/1 pint/2½ cups chicken
  stock
600ml/1 pint/2½ cups milk
30ml/2 tbsp medium pinhead
  oatmeal
25g/1oz butter
6 large leeks, washed and sliced
  into 2cm/¾in pieces
sea salt and black pepper
pinch of ground mace
30ml/2 tbsp chopped fresh parsley

Serves 4–6

NUTRITIONAL INFORMATION Energy 73kcal/305kJ; Protein 2.3g;
Carbohydrate 6.6g, of which sugars 2.2g; Fat 4.4g, of which saturates 2.3g;
Cholesterol 9mg; Calcium 28mg; Fibre 2.5g; Sodium 29mg

1 Bring the stock and milk to the boil over a medium heat and sprinkle in the oatmeal. Stir well to prevent lumps forming, and then simmer gently for 10–15 minutes.

2 Melt the butter in a separate pan and cook the leeks over a gentle heat until softened slightly, then add them to the oatmeal mixture. Simmer for a further 15–20 minutes, until the oatmeal is cooked. A little water can be added if it is too thick.

3 Season with salt, black pepper and mace, stir in the parsley and serve in warmed bowls.

BLUE CHEESE AND LEEK SOUP

PROBIOTIC

This is probiotic and prebiotic in one hit! Stir the cheese in at the end and reheat briefly if necessary but do not boil or you will destroy the good bacteria in it.

50g/2oz/¼ cup butter
30ml/2 tbsp sunflower oil
3 large leeks, washed and
    thinly sliced
15g/½oz/2 tbsp spelt flour
1.5 litres/2½ pints/6¼ cups
    chicken or vegetable stock
175g/6oz blue cheese, such as
    Roquefort or Dorset Blue Vinney
15ml/1 tbsp wholegrain mustard,
    or to taste
ground black pepper
snipped chives, to garnish
sourdough or wholemeal
    (whole-wheat) bread, to serve

Serves 6

NUTRITIONAL INFORMATION Energy 187Kcal/773kJ; Protein 5.6g; Carbohydrate 4.3g, of which sugars 1.9g; Fat 16.6g, of which saturates 8.6g; Cholesterol 32mg; Calcium 118mg; Fibre 1.8g; Sodium 407mg

1 Heat the butter and oil together in a large heavy pan and gently cook the leeks in it, covered, for 10–15 minutes, or until just softened but not brown. Add the flour and cook for 2 minutes, stirring constantly with a wooden spoon.

2 Gradually add the stock, stirring constantly and blending it in well. Season with some black pepper (don't add salt as the cheese will be salty). Bring the soup to the boil, reduce the heat, cover and simmer very gently for about 15 minutes.

3 Crumble in 115g/4oz of the cheese and the mustard. Stir gently until melted but do not boil. Check the seasoning and serve the soup garnished with the remaining crumbled cheese and some chopped chives, with fresh bread.

GARLIC AND BUTTERNUT SQUASH SOUP

This is a wonderful, richly flavoured dish bursting with prebiotics. Adding a spoonful of the hot and spicy tomato salsa gives bite and gut-pleasing oligosaccharides.

2 garlic bulbs, outer skin removed
75ml/5 tbsp olive oil
a few fresh thyme sprigs
1 large butternut squash, halved
    and seeded
2 onions, peeled and chopped
5ml/1 tsp ground coriander
1.2 litres/2 pints/5 cups vegetable
    or chicken stock
30–45ml/2–3 tbsp chopped fresh
    oregano or marjoram
sea salt and ground black pepper

For the salsa
4 large ripe tomatoes, halved
    and seeded
1 red (bell) pepper, halved
    and seeded
1 large fresh red chilli, halved
    and seeded
30–45ml/2–3 tbsp extra virgin
    olive oil
15ml/1 tbsp balsamic vinegar
2.5ml/½ tsp clear honey (optional)

Serves 4–5

NUTRITIONAL INFORMATION Energy 238kcal/986kJ; Protein 2.9g; Carbohydrate 11.9g, of which sugars 10.3g; Fat 20.2g, of which saturates 3.1g; Cholesterol 0mg; Calcium 79mg; Fibre 4.1g; Sodium 11mg

1 Preheat the oven to 220°C/425°F/Gas 7. Place the garlic bulbs on a piece of foil and pour over half the olive oil. Add the thyme sprigs then fold the foil around the garlic bulbs to enclose completely. Place the parcel on a baking sheet with the butternut squash and brush the squash with 15ml/1 tbsp of the remaining olive oil. Add the tomatoes, red pepper and fresh chilli for the salsa.

2 Roast the vegetables for 25 minutes, then remove the garlic, tomatoes, pepper and chilli. Reduce the temperature to 190°C/375°F/Gas 5 and cook the squash for 20–25 minutes more, or until the squash is tender.

3 Heat the remaining oil in a large, heavy pan and cook the onions and ground coriander gently for about 10 minutes, or until softened.

4 Meanwhile, make the salsa. Skin the pepper and chilli and process in a food processor or blender with the tomatoes and 30ml/2 tbsp olive oil. Transfer to a bowl and stir in the vinegar and seasoning to taste, adding the honey if necessary. Add the remaining oil if you think the salsa needs it.

5 Squeeze the roasted garlic out of its papery skin into the onions and scoop the squash out of its skin, adding it to the pan. Add the stock, 5ml/1 tsp salt and plenty of black pepper. Bring to the boil and simmer for 10 minutes.

6 Stir in half the oregano or marjoram and cool the soup slightly, then process it in a blender or food processor. Alternatively, press the soup through a fine sieve or strainer.

7 Reheat the soup without allowing it to boil, then taste for seasoning before ladling it into warmed bowls. Top each with a spoonful of salsa and sprinkle over the remaining chopped oregano or marjoram. Serve immediately.

CHUNKY TOMATO SOUP WITH NOODLES

PREBIOTIC

This glorious prebiotic soup is based on a Moroccan favourite. You can purée it, if you prefer, but I like it just as it is, finished off with a swirl of probiotic yogurt and finely chopped coriander. Garlic lovers may like to add a crushed garlic clove and a little salt to the yogurt. Serve with chunks of sourdough or wholemeal bread.

45–60ml/3–4 tbsp olive oil
3–4 cloves
2 onions, chopped
1 butternut squash, peeled, seeded and cut into small chunks
4 celery sticks, chopped
2 carrots, peeled and chopped
8 large, ripe tomatoes, skinned and roughly chopped
5–10ml/1–2 tsp clear honey
15ml/1 tbsp tomato purée (paste)
5–10ml/1–2 tsp ras el hanout
2.5ml/½ tsp ground turmeric
a big bunch of fresh coriander (cilantro), chopped, reserving a few sprigs for garnish
1.75 litres/3 pints/7½ cups vegetable stock
a handful dried egg noodles or capellini, broken into pieces
salt and ground black pepper
60–75ml/4–5 tbsp creamy yogurt and bread, to serve

Serves 4

COOK'S TIP
Ras el hanout is a Moroccan spice blend that Is readily available in supermarkets. It is a mixture of warming sweet carminative spices, including cinnamon, ginger, cardamom and turmeric.

NUTRITIONAL INFORMATION Energy 449kcal/1898kJ; Protein 12.2g; Carbohydrate 74.8g, of which sugars 27.8g; Fat 13.9g, of which saturates 2.7g; Cholesterol 15mg; Calcium 230mg; Fibre 14.2g; Sodium 159mg

1 In a deep, heavy pan, heat the oil and add the cloves, onions, squash, celery and carrots. Fry until they begin to colour, then stir in the tomatoes and honey. Add the tomatoes and cook until the water reduces and they begin to pulp.

2 Stir the tomato purée, ras el hanout, turmeric and chopped coriander into the pan.

3 Pour in the stock and bring the liquid to the boil. Reduce the heat and simmer for 30–40 minutes until the vegetables are very tender and the liquid has reduced a little.

4 Add the noodles or pasta to the soup and cook for a further 8–10 minutes, or until soft.

5 Season the soup to taste and ladle it into bowls. Spoon a swirl of yogurt into each one, garnish with the extra coriander and serve with freshly baked bread.

CAULIFLOWER AND PORCINI SOUP

Sour cream and mushrooms are classic soup ingredients, and this version adds prebiotic cauliflower topped with slices of porcini mushrooms, which have a wonderful flavour.

1 cauliflower, trimmed and cut
  into florets
1.5 litres/2½ pints/6¼ cups
  chicken stock
20g/¾oz/1½ tbsp butter
30ml/2 tbsp spelt flour
150ml/¼ pint/⅔ cup sour cream
115g/4oz/1½ cups fresh porcini (or
  chestnut) mushrooms, cleaned
  and thinly sliced
2 tarragon sprigs, leaves finely
  chopped
sea salt and black pepper

Serves 6

NUTRITIONAL INFORMATION Energy 123kcal/512kJ; Protein 5g; Carbohydrate 6g, of which sugars 3g; Fat 9g, of which saturates 5g; Cholesterol 22mg; Calcium 49mg; Fibre 2.1g; Sodium 441mg

1 Put the cauliflower in a large pan with the chicken stock and bring to the boil. Reduce to a simmer and cook for 10 minutes.

2 Put 15g/½oz/1 tbsp butter into a small pan and melt over gentle heat. Add the flour and stir to make a smooth roux. Add a ladle of the cooking liquid from the cauliflower to the roux and combine, then transfer to the pan with the cauliflower.

3 Bring to a simmer, stirring, then cook for 10 minutes. Remove from the heat and blend in a food processor until smooth. Return to the pan, stir in the sour cream and season to taste. Reheat gently but do not boil.

4 Meanwhile, melt the remaining butter in a frying pan and fry the sliced mushrooms until golden. Serve the soup in bowls, topped with slices of porcini mushroom and chopped tarragon.

HOT AND SWEET VEGETABLE SOUP

This interesting combination of hot, sweet and sour flavours makes for a soothing, nutritious soup. You get maximum benefits from the probiotics as they are not cooked.

1.2 litres/2 pints/5 cups vegetable
  stock
5–10ml/1–2 tsp Thai red curry
  paste
2 fresh or dried kaffir lime
  leaves, torn
30ml/2 tbsp orange blossom honey
juice of 1 lime
1 carrot, cut into thin batons
30ml/2 tbsp soy sauce
50g/2oz baby spinach leaves, any
  coarse stalks removed
225g/8oz block silken tofu, diced

Serves 4

NUTRITIONAL INFORMATION Energy 103kcal/434kJ; Protein 5.5g;
Carbohydrate 13.3g, of which sugars 12.8g; Fat 3.5g, of which saturates
0.4g; Cholesterol 0mg; Calcium 320mg; Fibre 0.7g; Sodium 769mg

1 Heat the stock in a large pan, then add the red curry paste. Stir constantly over a medium heat until the paste has dissolved. Add the lime leaves and honey and bring to the boil.

2 Add the lime juice and carrot to the pan. Reduce the heat and simmer for 5–10 minutes. Discard the lime leaves. Stir in the soy sauce.

3 Place the spinach and tofu in four individual serving bowls and pour the hot stock over. Serve immediately.

MISO BROTH WITH TOFU

This really boosts your good bacteria as it is brimming with probiotic ingredients: miso paste, soy sauce and tofu, plus prebiotic greens and alliums, topped off with the carminative effect of fresh ginger and star anise too!

1 bunch of spring onions
  (scallions) or 5 baby leeks
15g/½oz fresh coriander (cilantro),
  stalks and leaves separated
3 thin slices fresh root ginger
2 star anise
1 small dried red chilli
1.2 litres/2 pints/5 cups dashi stock
  or vegetable stock
225g/8oz pak choi (bok choy) or
  other Asian greens, thickly sliced
200g/7oz firm tofu, cut into
  2.5cm/1in cubes
60ml/4 tbsp red miso
30–45ml/2–3 tbsp tamari
  (Japanese soy sauce)
1 fresh red chilli, seeded and
  shredded (optional)

Serves 4

NUTRITIONAL INFORMATION Energy 64kcal/267kJ; Protein 6.9g; Carbohydrate 2.7g, of which sugars 2.3g; Fat 3g, of which saturates 0.4g; Cholesterol 0mg; Calcium 394mg; Fibre 1.6g; Sodium 617mg

1 Cut the coarse green tops off the spring onions or baby leeks and slice the rest of the spring onions or leeks finely on the diagonal. Place the coarse green tops in a large pan with the coriander stalks, fresh root ginger, star anise, dried chilli and dashi or vegetable stock.

2 Heat the mixture gently until boiling, then lower the heat and simmer for 10 minutes. Strain, discarding the flavourings, and return the stock to the pan. Reheat until simmering.

3 Add the green portion of the sliced spring onions or leeks to the soup with the pak choi or greens and cook for 2 minutes.

4 Coarsely chop the coriander leaves and stir most of them into the soup with the white part of the spring onions or leeks. Cook for 1 minute. Add the tofu.

5 Mix 45ml/3 tbsp of the miso with a little of the hot soup in a bowl, then stir it into the soup with the tamari. Do not reheat.

6 Taste the soup and add more miso or tamari, if necessary. While still hot, ladle the soup into warmed serving bowls. Sprinkle with the remaining coriander and the fresh red chilli, if using, and serve at once.

COOK'S TIP
For the best flavour try and use dashi rather than vegetable stock. Dashi powder is available in most Asian stores.

APPETIZERS AND LIGHT MEALS

These dishes are all ideal to have as light lunches or suppers but could also be served to start dinner parties or more elaborate meals. They are especially useful when you know the main course isn't going to contain many probiotics or prebiotics so you can 'up' your intake for the day. There are also some great dips that could be served with pre-dinner drinks for nutritious nibbles.

CHEESE AND YOGURT DIP

Feta is a probiotic cheese as it's pickled in brine for several months. So when it is mixed with yogurt, it makes a pretty good combination. Rather than the usual white flatbreads to serve with it, try wholemeal ones or toasted sourdough or even fingers of pumpernickel for a great probiotic experience!

250g/9oz feta cheese
about 250ml/9fl oz/generous 1 cup
   thick, live bio Greek (US
   strained plain) yogurt
30ml/2 tbsp olive oil
15ml/1 tbsp za'atar
crudités and fingers of lightly
   toasted wholemeal (whole-
   wheat) pitta breads, to serve

Serves 6

COOK'S TIP
Za'atar is a Middle Eastern spice blend, a delicious blend of oregano, thyme and marjoram along with sesame seeds and sumac – and sometimes other sweet spices, such as cumin and coriander.

NUTRITIONAL INFORMATION Energy 192kcal/797kJ; Protein 9.5g; Carbohydrate 2.3g, of which sugars 1.5g; Fat 16.7g, of which saturates 8.4g; Cholesterol 29mg; Calcium 217mg; Fibre 0g; Sodium 631mg

1 Drain the feta cheese and pat dry with kitchen paper. Place the feta in a bowl and mash it with a fork.

2 Beat enough of the Greek yogurt into the feta to form a smooth, thick paste. Spoon the mixture in a shallow dish and drizzle the olive oil over the top.

3 Sprinkle with the za'atar before serving with crudités and strips of lightly toasted wholemeal pitta breads.

OLIVE TAPENADE

Make sure you use traditionally preserved probiotic olives and remember that you can give this dish more prebiotics over and above the garlic it contains by serving it with wholemeal bread or toast, and crudités such as cherry tomatoes, chicory, edamame beans, celery sticks, asparagus tips and/or tiny broccoli or cauliflower florets.

350g/12oz pitted brined black
    olives
50g/2oz can anchovies, plus
    their oil
30ml/2 tbsp capers
1–2 crushed garlic cloves
5ml/1 tsp chopped fresh thyme
15ml/1 tbsp Dijon mustard
juice of ½ lemon
45ml/3 tbsp olive oil
warm sourdough or wholemeal
    (whole-wheat) toast, and/or
    crudités, to serve

Serves 4

NUTRITIONAL INFORMATION Energy 196kcal/806kJ; Protein 4.4g;
Carbohydrate 0.8g, of which sugars 0.3g; Fat 19.5g, of which saturates 2.9g;
Cholesterol 8mg; Calcium 102mg; Fibre 3.5g; Sodium 2571mg

1 Place the ingredients in a food processor and blend until smooth, stopping and scraping down the sides as necessary.

2 Turn the dip into a dish and chill slightly before serving. Spread on warm sourdough or wholemeal bread or toast and a selection of crudités.

COOK'S TIP
The tapenade will keep for several days in a pot covered with a layer of olive oil to exclude any air.

HUMMUS

This classic chickpea dip makes a tasty snack, appetizer or light meal that is rich in vegetable protein, fibre and prebiotics. Serve with toasted flatbreads and a selection of raw fruit and vegetable crudités for extra fibre, vitamin and mineral value.

150g/5oz/¾ cup dried chickpeas
juice of 2 lemons
2 garlic cloves, sliced
30ml/2 tbsp olive oil, plus extra for
    drizzling
pinch of cayenne pepper, plus a
    little for dusting
150ml/¼ pint/⅔ cup tahini
black pepper
flatbreads or oatcakes, cherry
    tomatoes, vegetable sticks, such
    as celery, carrots and (bell)
    peppers, or slices of apple
    tossed in lemon juice, to serve

Serves 4

NUTRITIONAL INFORMATION Energy 453Kcal/1887kJ; Protein 15.7g; Carbohydrate 32.1g, of which sugars 13.8g; Fat 30g, of which saturates 4.2g; Cholesterol 0mg; Calcium 345mg; Fibre 10.5g; Sodium 49mg

1 Put the chickpeas in a bowl, cover with plenty of cold water and leave to soak overnight.

2 Drain, place in a pan and cover with fresh water. Bring to the boil and boil rapidly for 10 minutes. Reduce the heat and simmer gently for about 1 hour until soft. Drain.

3 Process the chickpeas in a food processor or blender until smooth. Add the lemon juice, garlic, olive oil, cayenne pepper and tahini and blend until creamy. Season with pepper and transfer to a serving dish. Drizzle with a little extra olive oil and dust with a little cayenne, and serve with flatbreads.

CHIANG MAI DIP WITH STEAMED VEGETABLES   PREBIOTIC

In Thailand, steamed vegetables are often partnered with raw ones to create contrasting textures. By happy coincidence, it is an extremely healthy way to serve them, giving you masses of prebiotics and even some probiotics from the soy sauce.

For the vegetables
1 head broccoli, divided into florets
125g/4½oz green beans, trimmed
125g/4½oz asparagus, trimmed
½ cauliflower, divided into florets
8 baby corn cobs
125g/4½oz sugar snap peas
sea salt

For the dip
1 fresh green chilli, seeded
4 garlic cloves, peeled
4 shallots, peeled
2 tomatoes, halved
5 pea aubergines (eggplants)
30ml/2 tbsp lemon juice
30ml/2 tbsp soy sauce, plus extra,
    if necessary

Serves 4

NUTRITIONAL INFORMATION Energy 70kcal/295kJ; Protein 6.8g; Carbohydrate 8.1g, of which sugars 7.2g; Fat 1.4g, of which saturates 0.3g; Cholesterol 0mg; Calcium 73mg; Fibre 4.7g; Sodium 1005mg

1 Steam the broccoli, green beans, asparagus and cauliflower over boiling water for about 4 minutes, until just tender but still with some 'bite'. Transfer them to a bowl and add the corn cobs and sugar snap peas. Set aside.

2 Make the dip. Preheat the grill or broiler. Wrap the chilli, garlic cloves, shallots, tomatoes and pea aubergines in a foil package. Grill for 10 minutes, until the vegetables have softened, turning the package over once or twice.

3 Unwrap the foil and tip its contents into a mortar or food processor. Add the lemon juice, soy sauce and a little salt. Pound with a pestle or process to a fairly liquid paste. Taste and season with more soy sauce if necessary. Spoon the dip into individual bowls. Serve, surrounded by the vegetables.

GRAVADLAX WITH HORSERADISH

This Scandinavian speciality ferments the salmon in salt and some sugar. It is normally preserved using white sugar but we use honey, a great prebiotic that also adds an extra dimension of flavour. Choose very fresh, sustainably sourced salmon and freeze it for up to four hours before preparing it. Make sure all your utensils are scrupulously clean too.

For the fish
1kg/2¼lb piece of very fresh
   salmon fillet, skin on
75g/3oz/⅓ cup coarse sea salt
25g/1oz/2 tbsp clear honey
10ml/2 tsp ground white pepper
30ml/2 tbsp fresh lemon juice
105ml/7 tbsp chopped fresh dill
½ lemon, thinly sliced, plus extra
   to garnish
fresh dill sprigs, to garnish

For the dressing
250ml/8fl oz/1 cup sour cream
30ml/2 tbsp double (heavy) cream
45ml/3 tbsp prepared creamed
   horseradish sauce, or to taste
45ml/3 tbsp chopped fresh dill
salt and ground white pepper

Serves 8–10

NUTRITIONAL INFORMATION Energy 479kcal/1981kJ; Protein 26.2g; Carbohydrate 0.4g, of which sugars 0.3g; Fat 40.4g, of which saturates 6.4g; Cholesterol 113mg; Calcium 35mg; Fibre 0g; Sodium 169mg

1 Line a baking dish with a large piece of foil, clear film or plastic wrap that is slightly larger than the dish, leaving the ends overlapping the sides of the dish. Carefully remove any small pin bones from the salmon fillet using a pair of tweezers (this is called pin-boning).

2 Cut small nicks in the skin to allow the salt and seasonings to penetrate, then cut the fillet in half.

3 Stir together the salt, honey and pepper in a small bowl. Place one piece of salmon skin side down in the lined dish. Drizzle with lemon juice, rub with half the salt mixture and sprinkle with half the dill. Arrange the lemon slices on top.

4 Place the second fillet on a board and rub the flesh evenly with the remaining salt mixture, then sprinkle with the remaining dill.

5 Carefully lift the second fillet and place it over the fillet in the dish, turning it skin side up to make a 'sandwich'.

6 Wrap tightly in the foil or film and weight with a heavy pot or board. Chill for 48 hours, turning the fish twice daily. It is cured when it turns a bright red and the edges are slightly white.

7 Use a large sharp knife to cut the salmon into very thin slices to serve; discard the skin.

8 To make the dressing, stir together the sour cream, double cream, horseradish, dill, salt and pepper, and chill until ready to serve. Garnish both the horseradish cream and the salmon with dill sprigs.

SALT HERRING OPEN SANDWICHES

PROBIOTIC

This is a traditional way of serving matjas salt herring, which is so popular throughout Scandinavia. The sweet sharpness of the beetroot counteracts the slightly salty fish beautifully. It's easy to make your own version of salt herrings or you can buy them online. It makes a substantial appetizer or a delicious light lunch.

300g/11oz matjes herring fillet
  (or homemade salt herrings,
  see page 37)
150ml/¼ pint/½ cup sour cream
2.5ml/½ tsp creamed horseradish
15ml/1 tbsp pickled beetroot (red
  beet) juice from a jar
2.5ml/½ tsp dried dill
115g/4oz/½ cup pickled beetroot
  (beets), diced
250g/9oz/1 cup diced cucumber
25g/1oz/2 tbsp salted butter,
  softened
2 large or 4 small slices dark rye or
  pumpernickel bread
2 large or 4 smaller round
  (butterhead) lettuce leaves
2 hard-boiled eggs, cut into
  wedges
4 parsley sprigs
sea salt and black pepper

Serves 4

NUTRITIONAL INFORMATION Energy 346kcal/1437kJ; Protein 13.5g; Carbohydrate 15.4g, of which sugars 9.7g; Fat 25.9g, of which saturates 12.5g; Cholesterol 165mg; Calcium 114mg; Fibre 1.6g; Sodium 506mg

1 If using matjes herring, wash well under cold running water, pat dry on kitchen paper, then cut into 2cm/1in pieces, if necessary. If using homemade fillets in brine, simply drain and pat dry.

2 Combine the sour cream, horseradish, beetroot juice and dill in a mixing bowl.

3 Stir in the herring, beetroot and cucumber; toss to coat evenly with the dressing. Season with salt and pepper, then chill in the refrigerator until needed.

4 To make the open sandwiches, butter each slice of bread to the edges, then top with the lettuce leaves. If you used large slices of bread, cut each slice of bread in half.

5 Leaving a curl of lettuce visible on each slice, spoon on the herring salad. Arrange egg wedges on top of each sandwich. Season with salt and pepper. Tuck a parsley sprig under the egg.

SALAD ROLLS WITH PUMPKIN AND TOFU

PROBIOTIC

These rice paper rolls make a tangy and nutritious lunch dish, packed with probiotics and prebiotics. You put all the ingredients on the table in small bowls and let everyone make their own. Give each person their own little dish of fish sauce for dipping.

about 30ml/2 tbsp groundnut
    (peanut) or sesame oil
175g/6oz tofu, rinsed and dried
4 shallots, halved and sliced
2 garlic cloves, finely chopped
350g/12oz pumpkin flesh,
    cut into strips
1 carrot, cut into thin strips
15ml/1 tbsp soy sauce
3–4 green Thai chillies, seeded and
    finely sliced
1 small, crispy lettuce, torn
    into strips
1 bunch fresh basil, stalks removed
115g/4oz/⅔ cup roasted unsalted
    peanuts, chopped
100ml/3½fl oz/scant ½ cup hoisin
    sauce
20 dried rice wrappers
sea salt
Thai or Vietnamese fish sauce,
    for dipping

Serves 4–5

NUTRITIONAL INFORMATION Energy 402Kcal/1669kJ; Protein 14g; Carbohydrate 29g, of which sugars 13g; Fat 26g, of which saturates 5g; Cholesterol 0mg; Calcium 321mg; Fibre 4.1g; Sodium 0.4g

1 Heat a heavy pan and smear with a little oil. Place the block of tofu in the pan and sear on both sides. Transfer to a plate and cut into thin strips.

2 Heat 30ml/2 tbsp oil in the pan and stir in the shallots and garlic. Add the pumpkin and carrot, then pour in the soy sauce and 120ml/4fl oz/½ cup water. Add a little salt to taste and cook gently until the vegetables have softened slightly.

3 Meanwhile, arrange the tofu, chillies, lettuce, basil, roasted peanuts and hoisin sauce in separate dishes. Fill a bowl with hot water or fill a small bowl for each person, and place the stack of rice wrappers beside it. Tip the cooked vegetable mixture into a dish, and place everything on the table.

4 To eat, take a rice wrapper and dip it in the water for a few seconds to soften. Lay the wrapper flat on the table or on a plate and, just off-centre, spread a few strips of lettuce, some pumpkin, tofu, a sprinkling of chillies, a drizzle of hoisin sauce, basil leaves and peanuts, layering them in a stack. Pull the short edge of the wrapper up over the stack, tuck in the sides and roll into a tight cylinder. Dip the roll into fish sauce, before eating.

GRILLED LEEK AND COURGETTE SALAD

This salad makes a lovely summery appetizer or main course when served on a bed of crisp, sweet lettuce. It's predominantly prebiotic leeks, but you've got wonderful probiotic olives and feta cheese and some carminative mint and chilli too!

12 slender, baby leeks
6 small courgettes (zucchini)
45ml/3 tbsp extra virgin olive oil,
    plus extra for brushing
finely grated zest and juice of
    ½ lemon
1–2 garlic cloves, finely chopped
½ fresh red chilli, seeded
    and diced
50g/2oz/½ cup brined black olives,
    pitted and roughly chopped
30ml/2 tbsp chopped fresh mint
150g/5oz feta cheese, sliced
    or crumbled
sea salt and ground black pepper
fresh mint leaves, to garnish

Serves 6

NUTRITIONAL INFORMATION Energy 197kcal/812kJ; Protein 6.2g; Carbohydrate 3.4g, of which sugars 2.9g; Fat 17.6g, of which saturates 5.3g; Cholesterol 18mg; Calcium 140mg; Fibre 2.6g; Sodium 552mg

1 Bring a pan of water to the boil. Add the leeks and cook gently for 2–3 minutes.

2 Drain the leeks, refresh under cold water, then squeeze out any excess water and leave to drain.

3 Cut the courgettes in half lengthways. If time, place in a colander, adding 5ml/1 tsp salt to the layers, and leave to drain for about 45 minutes. Rinse well under running water and pat dry thoroughly on kitchen paper.

4 Heat the grill or broiler. Brush the leeks and courgettes lightly with oil. Grill the leeks for 2–3 minutes on each side and the courgettes for about 5 minutes on each side.

5 Place the grilled leeks in a shallow dish, together with the courgettes.

6 Place the remaining oil in a small bowl and whisk in the lemon zest, 15ml/1 tbsp of the lemon juice, the garlic and chilli. Season with salt and black pepper.

7 Pour the dressing over the leeks and courgettes. Stir in the olives and chopped mint, then set aside to marinate for a few hours, turning the vegetables once or twice.

8 If the salad has been marinating in the refrigerator, remove it 30 minutes before serving and bring back to room temperature. When ready to serve, add the feta cheese and garnish with several fresh mint leaves.

STUFFED MUSHROOMS WITH GARLIC CRUMBS   PROBIOTIC

Serve these succulent Stilton-stuffed mushrooms, a mixture of prebiotic and probiotic ingredients, with chunks of warm, crusty bread to mop up the sauce.

450g/1lb large mushrooms
3 garlic cloves, finely chopped
90g/3½oz butter, melted
juice of ½ lemon
115g/4oz Stilton cheese, crumbled
50g/2oz/½ cup chopped walnuts
90g/3½oz/1 cup fresh sourdough
    breadcrumbs
25g/1oz Parmesan cheese, grated
30ml/2 tbsp chopped fresh parsley
sea salt and black pepper

For the sauce
200ml/7fl oz/scant 1 cup live bio
    Greek (US strained plain) yogurt
5ml/1 tsp Dijon mustard
a handful mixed fresh herbs,
    chopped (such as chives,
    parsley, basil and tarragon)

Serves 4

NUTRITIONAL INFORMATION Energy 416kcal/1719kJ; Protein 13.3g; Carbohydrate 1.2g, of which sugars 0.8g; Fat 39.5g, of which saturates 20.6g; Cholesterol 88mg; Calcium 209mg; Fibre 2.2g; Sodium 514mg

1 Preheat the oven to 200°C/400°F/Gas 6. Place the mushrooms in an ovenproof dish and scatter half the garlic over them. Drizzle with 60ml/4 tbsp of the butter and the lemon juice. Season with salt and pepper and bake for 15 minutes.

2 Cream the crumbled Stilton with the chopped walnuts and mix in 30ml/2 tbsp of the breadcrumbs.

3 Stuff the mushrooms with the cheese mixture. Preheat the grill or broiler. Mix the remaining garlic, breadcrumbs and melted butter together. Stir in the Parmesan and parsley and season with pepper. Top the mushrooms with the breadcrumb mixture and grill for 5 minutes until crisp and browned.

4 Meanwhile, mix the yogurt with the mustard and herbs and spoon into a small serving dish. Serve the mushrooms straight from the grill with the yogurt sauce.

CHICKPEA AND BULGUR SALAD WITH MINT PREBIOTIC

This is a traditional Middle-Eastern salad, packed with prebiotics. It could be served as part of a mezze course, but also as a side dish to grilled meat, poultry or fish.

150g/5oz/scant 1 cup fine bulgur
   wheat, rinsed
400g/14oz canned chickpeas,
   drained and rinsed
1 red onion, finely chopped
15–30ml/1–2 tbsp toasted
   sesame seeds
2–3 garlic cloves, crushed
60–75ml/4–5 tbsp olive oil
juice of 1–2 lemons
bunch of flatleaf parsley,
   finely chopped
large bunch of mint, chopped
sea salt and black pepper
5ml/1 tsp paprika, to garnish
live bio Greek (US strained plain)
   yogurt and a tomato and onion
   salad, to serve

Serves 4

NUTRITIONAL INFORMATION Energy 267kcal/1116kJ; Protein 8.6g; Carbohydrate 34.1g, of which sugars 3.3g; Fat 11.4g, of which saturates 1.4g; Cholesterol 0mg; Calcium 89mg; Fibre 4.1g; Sodium 153mg

1 Place the bulgur in a bowl and pour over boiling water to cover. Soak for 10–15 minutes, until it has doubled in volume.

2 Meanwhile, place the chickpeas in a bowl with the onion, sesame seeds, garlic, olive oil and lemon juice.

3 Squeeze the bulgur to remove any excess water and add it to the chickpeas with the parsley and mint. Toss well, season with salt and pepper to taste, and sprinkle the paprika over the top. Serve with a good dollop of probiotic live bio yogurt and a tomato and onion salad.

COOK'S TIP
To toast sesame seeds, dry roast in a frying pan, over a low heat, stirring, until the seeds turn golden brown. Tip out of the pan immediately to prevent burning, and leave to cool.

SAUERKRAUT SALAD

PROBIOTIC

This is one of the best ways to serve sauerkraut so it retains all of its health benefits, and contains probiotic celery. Serve it on its own or as an accompaniment.

450g/1lb sauerkraut (see page 35)
115g/4oz/1 cup diced cooked
　beetroot (beets)
2 large carrots, peeled and grated
115g/4oz/1 cup diced cucumber
50g/2oz/½ cup diced celery
225g/8oz/2 cups diced
　cooked potatoes
6 gherkins, very finely chopped
60ml/4 tbsp chopped fresh parsley

For the dressing
75ml/2½fl oz/⅓ cup light olive oil
30ml/2 tbsp cider vinegar
5ml/1 tsp wholegrain mustard
sea salt and black pepper

Serves 4

NUTRITIONAL INFORMATION Energy 204kcal/844kJ; Protein 4.2g; Carbohydrate 17.4g, of which sugars 8.6g; Fat 13.4g, of which saturates 1.9g; Cholesterol 0mg; Calcium 122mg; Fibre 5.7g; Sodium 823mg

1 Drain the sauerkraut in a sieve or strainer, then roughly chop it into smaller pieces, if necessary. Put it in a bowl with all the grated or diced beetroot, carrots, cucumber, celery and potatoes, along with half of the chopped gherkins and half of the parsley. Gently mix together.

2 Whisk the oil, vinegar, mustard, and a little salt and pepper together in a small jug or pitcher or bowl with a fork, or shake well in a screw-top jar. Drizzle the mixture over the vegetables and toss well.

3 Transfer the salad to a serving bowl or platter and serve sprinkled with the remaining gherkins and parsley.

WATERCRESS, PEAR AND ROQUEFORT SALAD   PROBIOTIC

Rich, strong, probiotic Roquefort cheese is served here with pears for digestive-boosting soluble fibre, and watercress and walnuts packed with health-protecting phytonutrients.

For the salad
75g/3oz/½ cup shelled
   walnuts, halved
2 crisp pears, cored and sliced
15ml/1 tbsp lemon juice
150g/5oz/1 large bunch
   watercress, tough
   stalks removed
200g/7oz/scant 2 cups Roquefort
   cheese, cut into chunks

For the dressing
45ml/3 tbsp extra virgin olive oil
30ml/2 tbsp lemon juice
2.5ml/½ tsp clear honey
5ml/1 tsp Dijon mustard
sea salt and black pepper

Serves 6

NUTRITIONAL INFORMATION Energy 414kcal/1716kJ; Protein 14.4g; Carbohydrate 8.8g, of which sugars 8.6g; Fat 36g, of which saturates 11.9g; Cholesterol 38mg; Calcium 334mg; Fibre 2.9g; Sodium 632mg

1 Toast the walnuts in a dry frying pan for 2 minutes until golden, tossing frequently to prevent them burning.

2 Meanwhile, make the dressing. Place the olive oil, lemon juice, honey, mustard and seasoning in a bowl or screw-top jar. Stir or shake thoroughly to combine.

3 Toss the pear slices in the lemon juice, then place them in a bowl and add the watercress, walnuts and Roquefort. Pour the dressing over the salad, toss well and serve immediately.

QUINOA SPROUTED SEED SALAD

PROBIOTIC

Make the quinoa sprouts for this delicious salad by following the instructions on page 43. If you wish you can buy some ready-grown alfalfa sprouts and use those instead.

75g/3oz broccoli, cut into florets
half of 1 yellow and half of 1 red
    (bell) pepper, seeded and cut
    into thin strips
50g/2oz/½ cup cashew nuts
15ml/1 tbsp sesame oil
250g/9oz/1½ cups quinoa sprouts
    (from about 75g/3oz/½ cup
    quinoa)
115g/4oz/½ cup beansprouts
50g/2oz/scant ½ cup grated carrot

For the dressing
15ml/1 tbsp toasted sesame oil
15ml/1 tbsp mirin
15ml/1 tbsp soy sauce
ground black pepper

Serves 4

NUTRITIONAL INFORMATION Energy 203kcal/848kJ; Protein 7g; Carbohydrate 21g, of which sugars 7g; Fat 11g, of which saturates 2g; Cholesterol 0mg; Calcium 41mg; Fibre 2g; Sodium 269mg

1 In a small pan of boiling water, lightly steam the broccoli florets for around 2–3 minutes until soft but still slightly crisp.

2 Toss the pepper and nuts with the sesame oil on an ovenproof tray. Place under a medium grill or broiler for 5–6 minutes, until the nuts are brown and the peppers softened. Roughly crush the nuts with the end of a rolling pin.

3 Place the quinoa sprouts, beansprouts and grated carrot in a medium bowl, then add the broccoli, peppers and nuts.

4 Make the dressing by shaking the ingredients together in a screw-top jar, or whisking in a bowl. Pour the dressing over the salad, toss and divide between four dishes.

COLESLAW WITH BLUE CHEESE

PREBIOTIC

Packed with prebiotics, coleslaw here becomes a light meal in its own right (with some good wholemeal or sourdough bread) due to its probiotic blue cheese dressing.

For the dressing
45ml/3 tbsp mayonnaise
45ml/3 tbsp live bio Greek
    (US strained plain) yogurt
50g/2oz blue cheese,
    such as Stilton
15ml/1 tbsp lemon juice
    or cider vinegar

For the coleslaw
about 500g/1¼lb white cabbage
    (or half red and half white)
1 carrot
1 small red onion
2 small celery sticks (from near
    the centre of the head)
1 crisp eating apple
salt and black pepper
watercress sprigs, to garnish

Serves 4

....
NUTRITIONAL INFORMATION Energy 86kcal/359kJ; Protein 2.7g;
Carbohydrate 5.1g, of which sugars 4.8g; Fat 6.3g, of which saturates 1.9g;
Cholesterol 9mg; Calcium 78mg; Fibre 1.6g; Sodium 116mg
....

1 To make the dressing, put the mayonnaise and yogurt into a large bowl and crumble in the cheese. Stir well, adding a squeeze of lemon juice or cider vinegar and seasoning to taste.

2 Trim and shred the cabbage finely, grate the carrot, chop the onion finely and cut the celery into very thin slices. Core and dice the apple but do not peel.

3 Add the cabbage, carrot, onion, celery and apple to the bowl and toss until all the ingredients are well mixed and coated with the dressing.

4 Cover the bowl and chill for 2–3 hours or until ready to serve. Stir before serving, garnish with watercress.

MAIN DISHES

Whether you eat your main meal at lunchtime or in the evening, it's important that it is a balance of some protein, a good portion of starchy carbohydrates, plenty of vegetables and, ideally, some fruit too. If you haven't had any dairy during the day, perhaps add some live bio yogurt with a fruit dessert. These main courses are divided into those that are largely probiotic and those that are mostly prebiotic, but in many cases they are a mixture of the two for the best possible health benefits.

POLLOCK WITH ONIONS

Pollock is a more sustainable and less expensive alternative to cod or haddock. The flesh is firmer than cod and has a slightly pearly hue. It is full of flavour and a perfect partner for lightly caramelized prebiotic onions.

50g/2oz/½ cup spelt flour
675g/1½lb pollock fillet, skinned
   and cut into 4 serving portions
50g/2oz/4 tbsp butter
15ml/1 tbsp sunflower oil
3 large onions, sliced
5ml/1 tsp clear honey
200ml/7fl oz/scant 1 cup light
   chicken stock or water
sea salt and black pepper
steamed baby potatoes and a
   green vegetable such as wedges
   of lightly cooked Savoy
   cabbage, to serve

Serves 4

NUTRITIONAL INFORMATION Energy 298kcal/1247kJ; Protein 32.9g; Carbohydrate 16g, of which sugars 5g; Fat 11.8g, of which saturates 6.7g; Cholesterol 104mg; Calcium 52mg; Fibre 1.3g; Sodium 180mg

1 Preheat the oven to 180°C/350°F/Gas 4. Put the flour on a large plate and season with salt and pepper. Dip the fish portions in the flour to coat on both sides.

2 Heat a knob or pat of the butter and the oil in a large frying pan until the butter has melted and foams. Swirl it round the pan. Add the floured fish and fry it quickly on both sides until browned. Place the fish in an ovenproof dish.

3 Melt the remaining butter in the same pan, add the onions, season with salt and pepper and fry gently for 10 minutes until softened and golden brown, stirring frequently.

4 Add the honey to the pan, increase the heat and allow the onions to caramelize slightly, stirring all the time. Spread the onions over the fish.

5 Add the stock or water to the frying pan, stirring and scraping up any sediment, bring to the boil then pour over the fish and onions.

6 Bake in the oven for about 20 minutes, until the fish is tender. Serve with steamed baby potatoes and Savoy cabbage.

COOK'S TIP For added flavour, stir in 2.5ml/½ tsp smoked paprika to the onions at the end of caramelizing.

MACKEREL WITH GOOSEBERRY RELISH

PREBIOTIC

Mackerel and gooseberries work well together, with the tart gooseberries cutting through the rich oiliness of the mackerel – they're also great prebiotics!

4 whole mackerel, cleaned
60ml/4 tbsp olive oil
steamed new potatoes and green
  beans, to serve

For the relish
250g/9oz gooseberries, topped and
  tailed and roughly chopped
25g/1oz/2 tbsp clear honey
5ml/1 tsp wholegrain mustard
salt and black pepper

Serves 4

COOK'S TIP Turn the grill on well in advance as the fish need a fierce heat to cook quickly.

NUTRITIONAL INFORMATION Energy 576kcal/2390kJ; Protein 38.1g; Carbohydrate 8.4g, of which sugars 8.4g; Fat 43.5g, of which saturates 8.2g; Cholesterol 108mg; Calcium 43mg; Fibre 1.5g; Sodium 128mg

1 For the relish, place the gooseberries in a pan with 45ml/3 tbsp water and the honey and cook, stirring, until a thick, chunky purée forms. Add the mustard and season to taste.

2 Preheat the grill or broiler to high. Using a sharp knife, slash the fish two or three times down each side then season and brush with the olive oil. Grill the fish for about 4 minutes on each side until cooked.

3 Place the mackerel on warmed plates and spoon a little of the sauce on top. Serve with new potatoes and green beans and the remaining sauce handed separately.

SALMON WITH WHIPPED YOGURT SAUCE

This pretty dish is perfect for a summer lunch or light supper. The yogurt is lightly cooked, so loses a little of its probiotic goodness, but it's still very gut-friendly.

4 salmon fillets, about 300g/
    11oz each
30ml/2 tbsp flour
45ml/3 tbsp olive oil
4 egg whites
200ml/7fl oz/scant 1 cup thick live
    bio yogurt
2 egg yolks
small bunch of dill, finely chopped
salt and ground black pepper
green salad, to serve

Serves 4

NUTRITIONAL INFORMATION Energy 749kcal/3118kJ; Protein 69g; Carbohydrate 10g, of which sugars 4g; Fat 49g, of which saturates 9g; Cholesterol 256mg; Calcium 191mg; Fibre 90.3g; Sodium 339mg

1 Preheat the oven to 160°C/325°F/Gas 3. Dust the salmon fillets in the flour and season with salt and pepper.

2 Heat the olive oil in a non-stick frying pan. Sauté the salmon for 2 minutes on each side, or until cooked though. Remove and arrange in a flat ovenproof dish.

3 Put the egg whites into a clean, grease-free bowl and whisk until foamy. Put the yogurt and egg yolks in another bowl and mix to combine, season with salt and pepper and add the dill.

4 Fold the egg whites into the egg yolk mixture and pour over the salmon. Bake for 10 minutes. Serve with a green salad.

THAI PRAWN SALAD WITH FRIZZLED SHALLOTS PREBIOTIC

In this intensely flavoured salad, prawns and mango are partnered with a sweet-sour garlic dressing spiked with the hot taste of chilli. The crisp frizzled shallots are a traditional addition to Thai salads and add even more prebiotics along with the peanuts, onion and garlic. To make it more substantial, cook some jasmine rice (preferably brown) and put a spoonful on the plates before arranging the salad on top.

675g/1½lb medium raw prawns
    (shrimp), peeled and deveined,
    with tails intact
finely shredded rind of 1 lime
½ fresh red chilli, seeded and
    finely chopped
30ml/2 tbsp sunflower oil, plus
    extra for brushing
1 ripe but firm mango
2 carrots, cut into long thin shreds
10cm/4in piece cucumber, sliced
1 small red onion, halved and
    thinly sliced
a few fresh mint sprigs
a few fresh coriander
    (cilantro) sprigs
45ml/3 tbsp roasted, unsalted
    peanuts, coarsely chopped
4 large shallots, thinly sliced and
    fried until crisp in 30ml/2 tbsp
    groundnut (peanut) oil, and
    drained on kitchen paper
salt and black pepper

For the dressing
1 large garlic clove, chopped
10–15ml/2–3 tsp clear honey
juice of 2 limes
15–30ml/1–2 tbsp Thai fish sauce
1 fresh red chilli, seeded
    and finely chopped
5–10ml/1–2 tsp light rice vinegar

Serves 4–6

NUTRITIONAL INFORMATION Energy 292kcal/1222kJ; Protein 33.5g; Carbohydrate 13.4g, of which sugars 11.8g; Fat 11.9g, of which saturates 2g; Cholesterol 329mg; Calcium 160mg; Fibre 2.7g; Sodium 596mg

1 Make the dressing. Place the garlic in a mortar with 10ml/2 tsp of the honey. Pound with a pestle until smooth, then work in about three-quarters of the lime juice, followed by 15ml/1 tbsp of the Thai fish sauce.

2 Transfer the dressing to a jug or pitcher. Stir in half the chopped red chilli and a little light rice vinegar to taste. Taste the dressing and add more honey, lime juice and/or fish sauce if required. Cover and chill until ready to serve.

3 Place the prawns in a glass dish with the lime rind, chilli, oil and seasoning. Toss to mix and leave to marinate at room temperature for 30–40 minutes.

4 Peel and stone or pit the mango. The best way to do this is to cut either side of the large central stone, as close to it as possible, with a sharp knife. Cut the flesh into very fine strips and cut off any flesh still adhering to the stone.

5 Place the strips of mango in a bowl and add the carrots, cucumber slices and red onion. Pour over about half the dressing and toss thoroughly. Arrange the salad on four to six individual serving bowls.

6 Heat a ridged, cast-iron griddle pan or heavy frying pan until very hot. Brush with a little oil, then sear the marinated prawns for 2–3 minutes on each side, until they are pink and patched with brown on the outside. Arrange the prawns on the salads.

7 Sprinkle the remaining dressing over the salads and garnish with the mint and coriander sprigs. Sprinkle over the remaining chilli with the peanuts and crisp-fried shallots and serve.

CHICKEN TAGINE WITH OLIVES AND LEMON

PROBIOTIC

The olives and preserved lemon strips are added at the end of cooking to preserve their probiotic properties. To make your own preserved lemons see the recipe on page 39.

1.5kg/3lb oven-ready chicken
3 garlic cloves, crushed
juice of ½ lemon
2.5ml/½ tsp coarse sea salt
45–60ml/3–4 tbsp olive oil
1 large onion, grated
small bunch of fresh coriander
    (cilantro), finely chopped
pinch of saffron threads
5ml/1 tsp ground ginger
5ml/1 tsp ground black pepper
1 cinnamon stick
15ml/1 tbsp liquid from the
    preserved lemon jar
175g/6oz/1½ cups cracked
    green olives
2 preserved lemons, cut into strips
225g/8oz/1⅓ cups couscous
green salad, to serve

Serves 4

NUTRITIONAL INFORMATION Energy 474kcal/1967kJ; Protein 36.3g; Carbohydrate 5.3g, of which sugars 3.8g; Fat 34.3g, of which saturates 8.1g; Cholesterol 209mg; Calcium 83mg; Fibre 2.6g; Sodium 807mg

1 Place the chicken in a tagine or casserole. Rub the garlic, lemon juice and salt in the cavity. Mix the olive oil with the grated onion, coriander, saffron, ginger and pepper and rub all over the chicken. Cover and leave for about 30 minutes.

2 Pour in enough water to come halfway up the chicken, add the cinnamon stick and liquid from the preserved lemon jar and place on the hob. Bring to the boil, reduce the heat, cover and simmer for about 1 hour, turning the chicken occasionally.

3 Lift the chicken out of the tagine or casserole, place on a serving plate and cover with foil. Turn up the heat and boil the liquid for 5 minutes to reduce. Replace the chicken in the liquid and baste. Add the olives and preserved lemon strips. Make the couscous according to the packet directions.

4 Stir some of the sauce into the couscous. Serve the chicken with the couscous, the remaining sauce and a green salad.

CHICKEN WITH 40 CLOVES OF GARLIC

PREBIOTIC

Forty cloves of prebiotic garlic sound daunting but it isn't as the cooked garlic becomes smooth and creamy – and what a delicious way to boost your good gut bacteria growth!

½ lemon
a few fresh rosemary sprigs
1.5–1.75kg/3–4½lb oven-ready
  chicken
4 or 5 large heads of garlic
60ml/4 tbsp olive oil
sea salt and black pepper
steamed broad (fava) beans
  and spring onions (scallions),
  to serve

Serves 6

COOK'S TIPS
The tender broad beans and spring onions add a probiotic element to this meal.
 Rather than serving the cloves as they are, you could pop the flesh out of the skins and mash the cloves into the pan juices for an aromatic sauce.

....
NUTRITIONAL INFORMATION Energy 316kcals/1326k; Protein 40.1g; Fat 15.9g of which saturated fat 3.6g; Carbohydrate 3.4g of which Sugars 0.3g; Fibre 0.9g; Calcium 19mg
....

1 Preheat the oven to 190°C/375°F/Gas 5. Place the lemon half and the rosemary sprigs in the chicken. Separate three or four of the garlic heads into cloves and remove the papery husks, but do not peel. Slice the top off the other garlic head.

2 Heat the oil in a large flameproof casserole. Add the chicken, turning it in the hot oil to coat. Season and add all the garlic.

3 Cover the casserole with a sheet of foil, then the lid, to seal in the steam, and the flavour. Cook for about 1¼ hours until the chicken is cooked. To check, pierce the thickest part of the thigh with a skewer – the juices should run clear.

4 Serve the chicken with the garlic and pan juices separately, accompanied by steamed broad beans and spring onions.

DUCK LEGS WITH RED CABBAGE

This traditional German dish is usually served with potato dumplings. It's also good with potato gnocchi or steamed plain potatoes sprinkled with chopped parsley. Rich duck is the perfect vehicle for prebiotic red cabbage warmed with carminative spices.

4 or 8 duck legs, depending on size
15ml/1 tbsp sunflower oil
1 onion, chopped
10ml/2 tsp tomato purée (paste)
200ml/7fl oz/scant 1 cup red wine
sea salt and ground white pepper
chopped fresh parsley, to garnish
steamed potatoes, to serve

For the red cabbage
2 onions, chopped
30ml/2 tbsp sunflower oil
1 red cabbage, quartered, cored
   and finely sliced
100ml/3½fl oz/scant ½ cup red
   wine vinegar
15ml/1 tbsp clear honey
2 bay leaves
3 star anise
1 cinnamon stick
200ml/7fl oz/1 cup apple juice
2 apples, chopped
30ml/2 tbsp redcurrant jelly
5ml/1 tsp cornflour (cornstarch)

Serves 4

NUTRITIONAL INFORMATION Energy 958kcal/3961kJ; Protein 20.7g; Carbohydrate 32.7g, of which sugars 28.5g; Fat 79.8g, of which saturates 22.8g; Cholesterol 12mg; Calcium 122mg; Fibre 5.1g; Sodium 146mg

1 First make the cabbage. Heat the oil in a large pan and fry the onion for 2 minutes. Add the cabbage, vinegar, honey, spices and apple juice, bring to the boil, cover and simmer for 30 minutes.

2 Stir the apples and redcurrant jelly into the cabbage and cook for a further 45 minutes, adding more apple juice if necessary.

3 Towards the end of the cooking time, blend the cornflour with water and stir into the cabbage. Preheat the oven to 200°C/400°F/Gas 6.

4 While the cabbage is cooking, place the duck legs in a roasting pan, season and brush with the sunflower oil.

5 Roast in the oven for 20 minutes, then reduce the temperature to 160°C/325°F/Gas 3, add 250ml/8fl oz/1 cup water and cook for a further 40 minutes, basting from time to time. When the legs are cooked, lift them out and keep them warm.

6 Spoon off all but 15ml/1 tbsp of the duck fat from the roasting pan and add the onion. Stir in and cook on a medium heat until the onion is softened. Stir in the tomato purée, then deglaze the pan with the wine and cook, stirring, for another 2 minutes.

7 Serve the duck legs with the onion sauce poured over, garnished with parsley and accompanied by the red cabbage and steamed potatoes.

DUCK AND BROCCOLI STIR-FRY

Stir-frying is a great way of retaining nutrients. The prebiotic broccoli in this dish is joined by some probiotic fermented sauces, that cut through the richness of the duck.

2 skinless duck breasts
15ml/1 tbsp sesame oil
15ml/1 tbsp sunflower oil
4 garlic cloves, finely sliced
2.5ml/½ tsp dried chilli flakes
120ml/4fl oz/½ cup water
1 head broccoli, cut into
    small florets
15ml/1 tbsp Thai fish sauce
15ml/1 tbsp light soy sauce
torn coriander (cilantro) leaves and
    15ml/1 tbsp toasted sesame
    seeds, to garnish

Serves 4

NUTRITIONAL INFORMATION Energy 192kcal/798kJ; Protein 18.7g; Carbohydrate 2.7g, of which sugars 2.3g; Fat 12.9g, of which saturates 2.1g; Cholesterol 69mg; Calcium 104mg; Fibre 3.6g; Sodium 436mg

1 Cut the duck meat into bite-sized pieces. Heat the oils in a wok or large, heavy frying pan and stir-fry the duck and garlic over a medium heat for 3–4 minutes until it is golden brown, but don't let the garlic burn.

2 Stir in the chilli flakes and water. Add the broccoli and continue to stir-fry for about 2 minutes, until the duck is just cooked through and the broccoli is tender but still with some 'bite'. Add the Thai fish sauce and soy sauce. Toss well.

3 Serve on warmed plates, garnished with coriander and sesame seeds.

COOK'S TIP The stir-fry is good served with some udon (buckwheat) noodles, dressed in a little soy sauce and sunflower oil with a grating of carminative fresh ginger.

EGG NOODLE SALAD WITH SESAME CHICKEN   PROBIOTIC

This is a delicious, light fresh-tasting salad. To add some prebiotics, use dried whole-wheat noodles instead of egg noodles. Cook according to the packet.

400g/14oz fresh thin egg noodles
1 carrot, cut into long fine strips
50g/2oz mangetouts (snow peas),
    trimmed and cut into fine strips
115g/4oz/½ cup beansprouts
30ml/2 tbsp olive oil
225g/8oz chicken fillet, finely sliced
30ml/2 tbsp sesame seeds, toasted
2 spring onions (scallions), finely
    sliced, and fresh coriander
    (cilantro) leaves, to garnish

For the dressing
45ml/3 tbsp sherry vinegar
75ml/5 tbsp soy sauce
60ml/4 tbsp sesame oil
90ml/6 tbsp light olive oil
1 garlic clove, finely chopped
5ml/1 tsp grated fresh root ginger
ground black pepper

Serves 4–6

NUTRITIONAL INFORMATION Energy 546kcal/2286kJ; Protein 19.3g; Carbohydrate 50.9g, of which sugars 3.8g; Fat 30.9g, of which saturates 5.3g; Cholesterol 46mg; Calcium 69mg; Fibre 3.2g; Sodium 860mg

1 To make the dressing, whisk together all the ingredients in a small bowl. Season to taste with pepper.

2 Cook the noodles in a large pan of boiling water. Stir them occasionally to separate. They will take only a few minutes to cook. Drain, rinse under cold running water and tip into a bowl.

3 Add the carrot, mangetouts and beansprouts to the noodles. Pour in about half of the dressing, then toss the mixture well and adjust the seasoning according to taste.

4 Heat the oil in a large frying pan. Add the chicken and stir-fry for 3 minutes until cooked through. Remove from the heat. Add the sesame seeds and drizzle in some of the remaining dressing.

5 Arrange the noodle mixture in a nest on individual plates. Spoon the chicken on top. Sprinkle with the spring onions and coriander leaves and serve any remaining dressing separately.

BEEF STEW WITH STAR ANISE

This is a great way to eat probiotic beansprouts, popped raw in the bowls with the rich fragrant beef and broth spooned over. For a real probiotic hit serve with kimchi.

1 litre/1¾ pints/4 cups vegetable
   or chicken stock
450g/1lb beef steak, cut into strips
3 garlic cloves, finely chopped
3 coriander (cilantro) stalks,
   finely chopped
2 cinnamon sticks
4 star anise
30ml/2 tbsp light soy sauce
30ml/2 tbsp Thai fish sauce
5ml/1 tsp clear honey
3 nests of whole-wheat noodles
115g/4oz/1⅓ cups beansprouts
1 spring onion (scallion), chopped
small bunch fresh coriander
   (cilantro), coarsely chopped

Serves 4

NUTRITIONAL INFORMATION Energy 147kcal/615kJ; Protein 18.2g; Carbohydrate 2.8g, of which sugars 1.6g; Fat 7.1g, of which saturates 2.9g; Cholesterol 44mg; Calcium 11mg; Fibre 0.5g; Sodium 405mg

1 Pour the stock into a large, heavy pan. Add the beef, garlic, chopped coriander, cinnamon sticks, star anise, soy sauce, fish sauce and honey. Bring to the boil, then reduce the heat to low and simmer for 30 minutes. Skim off any foam that rises to the surface of the liquid with a slotted spoon.

2 Cook the noodles according to packet directions and drain. Divide the noodles among four individual warm serving bowls and top with the beansprouts.

3 Remove and discard the cinnamon sticks and star anise from the stew with a slotted spoon, if liked. Ladle the stew over the beansprouts and noodles, garnish with the chopped spring onion and chopped fresh coriander and serve immediately.

LAMB BURGERS STUFFED WITH BLUE CHEESE   PROBIOTIC

The blue cheese and crème fraîche give these burgers a creamy consistency. Some probiotics will be lost in the cooking, but they will still encourage good healthy gut flora.

2 potatoes, cooked whole in their skins and drained
60ml/4 tbsp milk
15g/½oz/1 tbsp butter
1 egg, beaten
1 red onion, chopped
100ml/4fl oz/½ cup crème fraîche
15ml/1 tbsp mustard seeds
400g/14oz minced (ground) lamb
225g/8oz/1 cup blue cheese such as Gorgonzola or Stilton, cut in 8 pieces
sea salt and black pepper
a little sunflower oil for brushing
mashed potatoes and steamed cabbage, to serve

Serves 4

NUTRITIONAL INFORMATION Energy 641kcal/2667kJ; Protein 36.8g; Carbohydrate 21.2g, of which sugars 4.7g; Fat 46g, of which saturates 26.5g; Cholesterol 247mg; Calcium 360mg; Fibre 2g; Sodium 824mg

1 Peel the potatoes and place in a bowl, add the milk and butter and mash the potatoes well. Add the egg, chopped onion, crème fraîche, mustard seeds, salt and pepper and mix well together. Add the lamb and mix again.

2 Form the mixture into 16 round, flat burgers. Put a piece of blue cheese on the centre of 8 of the burgers and then place the remaining burgers on top to make 8 larger burgers. Press the edges well together to seal.

3 Preheat the grill or broiler. Place the burgers in the rack, set about 5cm/2in from the heat source, and brush with a little oil. Grill for 3–4 minutes on each side, until golden and the cheese has just melted. Serve hot with mashed potato and cabbage.

LAMB KEBABS WITH SALSA

PREBIOTIC

Kebabs are always popular with family members. The meat is marinated in carminative spices and served with a great prebiotic and probiotic salsa. You could add some diced avocado and some diced dried apricots to the salsa for their health-boosting antioxidant properties and added fibre – and the fact that they taste wonderful.

2 garlic cloves, crushed
60ml/4 tbsp lemon juice
30ml/2 tbsp olive oil
2.5ml/½ tsp dried chilli flakes
5ml/1 tsp ground cumin
5ml/1 tsp ground coriander
500g/1¼lb lean lamb,
   cut into cubes
1 yellow and 1 red (bell) peppers,
   seeded and cut into chunks
8–12 small shallots, peeled
sea salt and black pepper
warm flatbreads and yogurt
   sprinkled with sumac, to serve

For the tomato salsa
175g/6oz/1½ cups mixed pitted
   green and black olives in brine,
   roughly chopped
1 small red onion, finely chopped
4 tomatoes, skinned and
   finely chopped
1 red chilli, seeded and
   finely chopped
30ml/2 tbsp olive oil

Serves 4

NUTRITIONAL INFORMATION Energy 394kcal/1636kJ; Protein 28.3g; Carbohydrate 11.8g, of which sugars 10.5g; Fat 27.2g, of which saturates 6.9g; Cholesterol 93mg; Calcium 102mg; Fibre 5.5g; Sodium 1089mg

1 Mix the garlic, lemon juice, olive oil, chilli, cumin and coriander together in a large shallow dish. Add the lamb cubes, with some salt and a good grinding of pepper. Mix well. Cover and leave to marinate in a cool place for 2 hours.

2 Make the salsa. Put the olives, onion, tomatoes, chilli and olive oil in a bowl. Stir in salt and pepper to taste. Mix well, cover and set aside. Light the barbecue, grill or broiler.

3 Remove the lamb from the marinade and divide the cubes among four skewers, threading on the pieces of yellow and red pepper and shallots at intervals.

4 Cook on the hot coals of the barbecue, on a ridged griddle pan or under the hot grill, turning occasionally, for 10 minutes, until the lamb is browned and crisp on the outside and pink and juicy inside.

5 Serve the kebabs with the salsa, warm flatbreads and a dollop of yogurt sprinkled with sumac.

TOFU AND GREEN BEAN RED CURRY

The tofu in this curry takes on the flavour of the spice paste and brings its probiotic properties to the dish along with protein, calcium, vitamins and minerals.

600ml/1 pint/2½ cups canned
   coconut milk
15ml/1 tbsp Thai red curry paste
45ml/3 tbsp Thai fish sauce
10ml/2 tsp clear honey
225g/8oz/3¼ cups button
   (white) mushrooms
115g/4oz green beans, trimmed
175g/6oz firm tofu, rinsed, drained
   and cut in 2cm/¾in cubes
4 kaffir lime leaves, torn
2 fresh red chillies, seeded
   and sliced
coriander (cilantro) leaves,
   to garnish

Serves 4

NUTRITIONAL INFORMATION Energy 59kcal/250kJ; Protein 3.8g; Carbohydrate 7.5g, of which sugars 7.1g; Fat 1.8g, of which saturates 0.4g; Cholesterol 0mg; Calcium 188mg; Fibre 0.8g; Sodium 291mg

1 Pour about one-third of the coconut milk into a wok or pan. Cook until it starts to separate and an oily sheen appears on the surface. Add the red curry paste, fish sauce and honey to the coconut milk. Mix thoroughly, then add the mushrooms. Stir and cook for 1 minute.

2 Stir in the remaining coconut milk. Bring back to the boil, then add the green beans. Simmer gently for 4–5 minutes more. Remove from the heat.

3 Stir in the tofu, kaffir lime leaves and sliced red chillies. Cover with a lid and foil to keep it hot and leave to stand for 5 minutes to infuse before serving. Garnish with coriander.

POTATO CURRY WITH YOGURT

Although classed as a probiotic dish, because of the yogurt stirred in, this curry has also great prebiotics: lots of garlic, some shallots and tomatoes, as well as carminative spices.

6 garlic cloves, chopped
25g/1oz fresh root ginger, grated
15ml/1 tbsp sunflower oil
15g/½oz/1 tbsp butter
6 shallots, sliced
2 green chillies, seeded and
    finely sliced
10ml/2 tsp clear honey
a handful of fresh or dried
    curry leaves
2 cinnamon sticks
5–10ml/1–2 tsp ground turmeric
15ml/1 tbsp garam masala
600g/1lb 6oz waxy potatoes,
    cut into bite-size pieces
2 tomatoes, skinned seeded
    and quartered
250ml/8fl oz/1 cup live bio Greek
    (US strained plain) yogurt
5ml/1 tsp red chilli powder, and
    fresh coriander (cilantro) and
    mint leaves, finely chopped
sea salt and ground black pepper
1 lemon, quartered, wholemeal
    (whole-wheat) chapattis and a
    crisp mixed salad including
    chopped fresh mango and
    sliced red onion, to serve

Serves 4

NUTRITIONAL INFORMATION Energy 231Kcal/967kJ; Protein 6.7g; Carbohydrate 26.2g, of which sugars 7.4g; Fat 12.4g, of which saturates 4.1g; Cholesterol 0mg; Calcium 110mg; Fibre 2g; Sodium 63mg

1 Using a mortar and pestle grind the garlic and ginger to a coarse paste. Heat the oil and butter in a heavy pan and stir in the shallots and chillies for about 30 seconds until fragrant. Stir in the garlic paste and honey. Add the curry leaves, cinnamon sticks, turmeric and garam masala, and toss in the potatoes, making sure they are coated in the spice mixture.

2 Pour in just enough cold water to cover the potatoes. Bring to the boil, reduce the heat and simmer until the potatoes are tender. Season with salt and pepper to taste.

3 Gently toss in the tomatoes to heat them through. Fold in the yogurt so that it is streaky rather than completely mixed in. Sprinkle with the chilli powder, coriander and mint. Serve from the pan, with lemon to squeeze over, chapattis for scooping it up and a crisp mixed salad including mango and red onion.

BRIE AND BLACK OLIVE TART

The olives and Brie are cooked so their probiotic properties won't be as great, but they will still encourage the growth of good bacteria, as will the prebiotic spelt pastry.

3 eggs, beaten
300ml/½ pint/1¼ cups milk
30ml/2 tbsp chopped fresh herbs,
    such as parsley, marjoram
    or basil
6 firm plum tomatoes, sliced
75g/3oz ripe Brie cheese, cubed
about 16 brined black olives,
    pitted and sliced
salt and black pepper

For the pastry
225g/8oz spelt flour
pinch of sea salt
150g/5oz cold butter, diced

Serves 8

NUTRITIONAL INFORMATION Energy 315kcal/1316kJ; Protein 9.3g; Carbohydrate 26.1g, of which sugars 4.6g; Fat 19.9g, of which saturates 7.2g; Cholesterol 90mg; Calcium 151mg; Fibre 1.7g; Sodium 505mg

1 For the pastry, mix the flour and salt in a bowl. Add the butter and rub in with the fingertips until the mixture resembles breadcrumbs. Mix with cold water to form a firm dough.

2 Preheat the oven to 190°C/375°F/Gas 5. Roll the pastry out thinly and use to line a 28 x 18cm/11 x 7in rectangular tart tin or pie pan, trimming off the edges. Chill for 20 minutes.

3 Line the pastry case or pie shell with baking parchment and baking beans, and bake blind for 15 minutes. Remove the baking parchment and beans and bake for 5 minutes until crisp.

4 Mix together the eggs, milk, seasoning and herbs. Place the cooled pastry case on a baking sheet, arrange the tomatoes, cheese and olives in the bottom, then pour in the egg mixture. Bake for 40 minutes until just firm. Serve warm, in slices.

BUTTER BEAN STEW

Butter beans are packed with vegetable protein as well as being prebiotic. They're floury enough to absorb lots of other strong flavours, including carminative spices too.

450g/1lb/2½ cups dried butter (lima) beans, soaked overnight
30ml/2 tbsp olive oil
a knob (pat) of butter
2 onions, finely chopped
4–6 garlic cloves, crushed
10ml/2 tsp clear honey
10ml/2 tsp ground cumin
10ml/2 tsp ground coriander
1 large cinnamon stick
2 x 400g/14oz cans chopped tomatoes
small bunch of fresh coriander (cilantro), coarsely chopped
sea salt and black pepper
live bio yogurt, sourdough bread and green salad, to serve

Serves 4–6

NUTRITIONAL INFORMATION Energy 295kcal/1251kJ; Protein 18.8g; Carbohydrate 45.4g, of which sugars 11.5g; Fat 5.7g, of which saturates 0.9g; Cholesterol 0mg; Calcium 108mg; Fibre 14.1g; Sodium 29mg

1 Drain the beans and transfer them to a pan filled with water. Bring to the boil, and boil rapidly for 10 minutes to destroy any toxins, then reduce the heat and simmer the beans for about 45 minutes, until they are tender but retaining a little bite. Drain, refresh in cold water, and remove any loose skins.

2 Heat the oil and butter in a heavy pan and cook the onions, garlic and honey for 2–3 minutes, until the onions begin to colour. Add the spices and toss in the beans. Add the tomatoes and simmer over a low heat for about 20 minutes until thick.

3 Season with salt and pepper and stir in half the fresh coriander. Remove the cinnamon and transfer the beans into a serving bowl. Garnish with the remaining coriander and serve with a dollop of yogurt, sourdough bread and a green salad.

SIDE DISHES

Side dishes and accompaniments are a brilliant
way to add probiotics and prebiotics to your diet
without spending time on complicated recipes.
Having a little dish of something sharp and tasty
alongside some simply pan-fried or grilled meat,
fish or chicken (or thick slices of halloumi cheese)
can turn any of them into a sumptuous, easy and
really nutritious meal.

SPINACH WITH YOGURT

This great probiotic and prebiotic dish is delicious served as an accompaniment to grilled meats, chicken or fish, or with kebabs. It's also good as a snack or light meal with some wholemeal flatbreads and, perhaps, topped with poached eggs.

500g/1¼lb fresh spinach, washed and drained
15–30ml/1–2 tbsp olive oil
1 onion, chopped
5ml/1 tsp ground cinnamon
5ml/1 tsp paprika
5ml/1 tsp ground cumin
small bunch of fresh coriander (cilantro), finely chopped
15–30ml/1–2 tbsp flaked (sliced) almonds
2 wholemeal (whole-wheat) pitta breads, toasted
15g/½oz/1 tbsp butter
15–30ml/1–2 tbsp pine nuts
sea salt and black pepper

For the yogurt sauce
600ml/1 pint/2½ cups live bio Greek (US strained plain) yogurt
2 garlic cloves, crushed
30ml/2 tbsp tahini
juice of ½ lemon

Serves 4

NUTRITIONAL INFORMATION Energy 435kcal/1818kJ; Protein 19.3g; Carbohydrate 45.1g, of which sugars 20g; Fat 21.3g, of which saturates 4.8g; Cholesterol 11mg; Calcium 625mg; Fibre 5.9g; Sodium 529mg

1 To prepare the yogurt sauce, beat the yogurt with the garlic, tahini and lemon juice and season it to taste with salt and pepper. Set aside.

2 Put the spinach in a steamer or a large pan with no extra water and cook for a minute or two until just wilted, stirring gently. Refresh under cold running water, drain and squeeze out the excess water. Chop the spinach coarsely.

3 Heat the oil in a heavy pan, stir in the onion and cook for 2–3 minutes. Stir in the spices and cook for 30 seconds until fragrant, stirring all the time. Add the spinach, making sure all the leaves are thoroughly mixed with the spiced oil.

4 Cook for a further 2–3 minutes until the spinach is wilted and bathed in the spicy mixture. Season well with salt and pepper. Mix in the fresh coriander and flaked almonds.

5 Break the toasted pitta bread into bite-sized pieces and arrange them in a serving dish. Spread the spinach over the top of the bread and spoon the yogurt sauce over the spinach.

6 Quickly melt the butter in a frying pan and add the pine nuts. Stir-fry until the pine nuts are golden in colour. Drizzle the butter from the pan over the yogurt and sprinkle the pine nuts on top. Serve immediately while the spinach is still warm.

STIR-FRIED BROCCOLI WITH SOY SAUCE

PREBIOTIC

Purple sprouting broccoli has been used for this recipe, but a head of calabrese will also work. Broccoli is a great prebiotic and packed with beta-carotene (for vitamin A), vitamin C and antioxidant properties that protect the immune system. Stir-frying is a good way to cook it as little vitamin C is lost when compared with cooking in water.

450g/1lb purple sprouting broccoli
30ml/2 tbsp olive oil
30ml/2 tbsp soy sauce
30ml/2 tbsp toasted sesame seeds
ground black pepper

Serves 4

NUTRITIONAL INFORMATION Energy 270kcal/1115kJ; Protein 13.1g; Carbohydrate 5.4g, of which sugars 4.6g; Fat 21.7g, of which saturates 3.3g; Cholesterol 0mg; Calcium 229mg; Fibre 7.1g; Sodium 1089mg

1 Using a sharp knife, cut off and discard any thick stems from the broccoli and cut the broccoli into long, thin florets.

2 Heat the olive oil in a wok or large frying pan and add the broccoli. Stir-fry for 3–4 minutes, or until tender, adding a splash of water if the pan becomes too dry.

3 Add the soy sauce to the broccoli, then season with black pepper to taste. Add sesame seeds, toss to combine and serve.

WILTED KALE WITH MUSTARD DRESSING PREBIOTIC

Kale is a wonderful prebiotic vegetable packed with nutrients such as potassium, beta-carotene (for vitamin A), vitamin C, vitamin B6, iron, magnesium and loads of gut-friendly fibre. To retain these nutrients blanch it for strictly 1 minute until wilted, to release all its delicious flavour while keeping as much of its goodness as possible.

250g/9oz curly kale, washed and
    drained, thick stalks removed
    and cut into large chunks
45ml/3 tbsp light olive oil
5ml/1 tsp wholegrain mustard
15ml/1 tbsp white wine vinegar
2.5ml/½ tsp clear honey
sea salt and black pepper

Serves 4

NUTRITIONAL INFORMATION Energy 99kcal/409kJ; Protein 2.1g; Carbohydrate 1.9g, of which sugars 1.9g; Fat 9.3g, of which saturates 1.3g; Cholesterol 0mg; Calcium 82mg; Fibre 2g; Sodium 27mg

1 Bring a large pan with about 5cm/2in water to the boil. Drop in the kale, press it down well, bring back to the boil then boil for 1 minute only until all the leaves are bright green and have wilted very slightly. Drain and rinse very briefly under the cold tap to refresh then drain again.

2 Whisk the oil into the mustard in a salad bowl. When it is blended completely, whisk in the white wine vinegar. It should begin to thicken.

3 Season the mustard dressing to taste with honey, sea salt and black pepper. Toss the kale in the dressing and serve.

CELERY IN TOMATO SAUCE

PREBIOTIC

Wonderful prebiotic celery takes on a gentler flavour when cooked, and here it's teamed with two other great good bacteria encouragers – tomatoes and garlic. This dish is delicious with fish or chicken, or great for a snack meal topped with poached eggs.

1 head of white celery, separated
  into sticks, leaves reserved
45ml/3 tbsp olive oil
3 garlic cloves, chopped
1 onion, chopped
2 x 400g/14oz cans plum
  tomatoes, drained and
  strained or use 800ml/
  generous 1¼ pints/3 cups
  passata (bottled strained
  tomatoes)
sea salt and black pepper

Serves 4

NUTRITIONAL INFORMATION Energy 115kcal/480kJ; Protein 1.7g; Carbohydrate 7.6g, of which sugars 7.2g; Fat 8.9g, of which saturates 1.4g; Cholesterol 0mg; Calcium 26mg; Fibre 2.4g; Sodium 31mg

1 Trim the celery sticks, removing any tough strings (I use a vegetable peeler). Cut into chunks and place in a bowl. Chop the leaves finely and set them aside in a separate bowl.

2 Heat the olive oil in a wide, shallow pan and add the garlic and onion. Cook for 3–4 minutes, until the onion has softened but not browned.

3 Stir in the celery chunks. Cook for 5 minutes. Pour in the tomatoes, stir and season to taste. Cover the pan and simmer for about 15 minutes or until the celery is soft. Stir in the chopped celery leaves, spoon the mixture into a dish and serve.

JERUSALEM ARTICHOKES GRATIN

PREBIOTIC

Jerusalem artichokes are not related to globe artichokes, but to the sunflower, which is why they're sometimes called 'sunchokes'. They are packed with prebiotics and have a nutty, earthy flavour. Here they are teamed with prebiotic sour cream and Cheddar.

675g/1½lb Jerusalem artichokes, coarsely chopped
250ml/8fl oz/1 cup sour cream
50ml/2fl oz/¼ cup single (light) cream
50g/2oz/½ cup grated aged Cheddar cheese
60ml/4 tbsp fresh breadcrumbs (preferably sourdough)
sea salt

Serves 4

NUTRITIONAL INFORMATION Energy 296kcal/1230kJ; Protein 6.9g; Carbohydrate 27.6g, of which sugars 15.5g; Fat 18.1g, of which saturates 11.1g; Cholesterol 52mg; Calcium 186mg; Fibre 4.4g; Sodium 240mg

1 Preheat the oven to 190°C/375°F/Gas 5. Lightly grease an ovenproof dish. Place the Jerusalem artichokes in a large bowl. Add the sour cream and single cream, and a pinch of salt. Toss to coat the artichokes.

2 Spread the artichokes in the prepared dish, and sprinkle with the cheese and breadcrumbs. Bake for about 30 minutes, until the cheese melts and the top is brown and bubbling.

BRAISED JERUSALEM ARTICHOKES

PREBIOTIC

Jerusalem artichokes are one of the top prebiotic foods. They can cause flatulence in some people (particularly if you are new to eating plenty of prebiotics and fibre) so it's a good idea to eat some live bio yogurt at the same time or soon after. The flavour is sumptuous though, especially when they are cooked in this rich tomato sauce. Eat as an accompaniment to grilled or roasted meat and poultry dishes – the dish is particularly delicious with roasted game.

500g/1¼lb Jerusalem artichokes
30–45ml/2–3 tbsp olive oil
2 onions, finely chopped
2 garlic cloves, finely chopped
2 x 400g/14oz cans chopped
   tomatoes
10–15ml/2–3 tsp clear honey
sea salt and black pepper
small bunch of fresh coriander
   (cilantro), finely chopped,
   to garnish
1 lemon, cut into wedges, to serve

Serves 4

NUTRITIONAL INFORMATION Energy 147kcal/619kJ; Protein 3.6g; Carbohydrate 19.8g, of which sugars 17g; Fat 6.6g, of which saturates 1g; Cholesterol 0mg; Calcium 98mg; Fibre 5.1g; Sodium 9mg

1 Peel the Jerusalem artichokes and cut them into bite-size pieces. This can be fiddly, and because they brown quickly you might want to drop them, when peeled, into a bowl of cold water with half a lemon squeezed in, while you work.

2 Heat the oil in a heavy pan, stir in the onions and cook until they begin to colour. Add the garlic and the pieces of artichoke, and toss well to make sure they are coated in the oil.

3 Add the tomatoes with the honey, cover the pan and cook gently for 25–30 minutes, until the artichokes are tender.

4 Remove the lid, bring to the boil and boil rapidly for a few minutes to reduce it a little.

5 Season with salt and pepper and transfer to a serving dish. Garnish with some coriander and serve with wedges of lemon to squeeze over the dish.

CATALAN-STYLE ROASTED VEGETABLES

PREBIOTIC

This combination of prebiotic vegetables makes a richly-flavoured accompaniment to just about any grilled meat, fish or poultry. I love it, too, simply topped with a poached egg and served with some warm sourdough bread. Pop the cooked garlic out of its skin and spread it on the bread or mash into the vegetable juices.

2 fairly large courgettes (zucchini)
6 whole garlic cloves, unpeeled
1 large fennel bulb, trimmed and
   cut into large wedges
1 large onion, peeled and cut
   lengthways into large wedges
2 large red (bell) peppers, seeded
   and sliced thickly lengthways
450g/1lb butternut squash, peeled
   and cut into large pieces
75ml/5 tbsp olive oil
juice of ½ lemon
pinch of cumin seeds, crushed
4 sprigs fresh thyme
4 tomatoes, quartered
salt and ground black pepper

Serves 4

NUTRITIONAL INFORMATION Energy 75kcal/313kJ; Protein 1.3g; Carbohydrate 7.5g, of which sugars 7.2g; Fat 3.9g, of which saturates 0.6g; Cholesterol 0mg; Calcium 17mg; Fibre 2g; Sodium 151mg

1 Preheat the oven to 220°C/425°F/Gas 7. Cut the courgettes in half widthways then lengthways and lightly crush the garlic cloves. Choose a roasting pan into which all the vegetables will fit in one layer. Put in all the vegetables except the tomatoes.

2 Mix together the oil and lemon juice, then pour over the vegetables and toss well.

3 Sprinkle the vegetables with the cumin seeds, salt and pepper and tuck in the thyme sprigs. Roast for 20 minutes.

4 Gently stir and turn the vegetables and add the tomatoes. Cook for a further 15 minutes, or until the vegetables are tender and slightly charred around the edges.

POTATO, ONION AND GARLIC GRATIN

This tasty side dish makes the perfect accompaniment to family roasts and casseroles. Although there is a lot of garlic and onions (so are a good prebiotic addition), they lose their acridity and become sweet and tender cooked this way, and the potatoes add a delicious creaminess.

40g/1½oz/3 tbsp butter
2 large onions, finely sliced
  into rings
4 garlic cloves, finely chopped
2.5ml/½ tsp dried thyme
900g/2lb waxy potatoes, scrubbed
  but not peeled, very finely sliced
450ml/¾ pint/2 cups boiling
  vegetable stock
sea salt and ground black pepper

Serves 4

NUTRITIONAL INFORMATION Energy 260Kcal/1092kJ; Protein 5.1g; Carbohydrate 41.9g, of which sugars 6.4g; Fat 9.1g, of which saturates 5.4g; Cholesterol 21mg; Calcium 31mg; Fibre 3.3g; Sodium 171mg

1 Preheat the oven to 200°C/375°F/Gas 5. Grease the inside of a shallow ceramic baking dish with butter. Spoon a thin layer of onions on to the base of the dish, then sprinkle over a little chopped garlic, thyme, salt and pepper.

2 Arrange an overlapping layer of potato slices on top of the onion mixture in the dish. Continue to layer the ingredients until all the onions, garlic, herbs and potatoes are used up, finishing with a layer of sliced potatoes and some seasoning.

3 Pour just enough of the stock into the dish to cover the potatoes. Cover tightly with foil and bake in the oven for about 1 hour or until the potatoes are tender. Remove the foil and cook for a further 15 minutes to brown the top. Serve hot.

THAI ASPARAGUS

This is an excitingly different way of cooking prebiotic asparagus. The crunchy texture is retained and the flavour is complemented by spices and probiotic soy and fish sauces.

350g/12oz asparagus spears
   (not too thick)
30ml/2 tbsp sunflower oil
1 garlic clove, peeled and crushed
15ml/1 tbsp sesame seeds
2.5cm/1in piece fresh galangal
   or fresh root ginger, peeled
   and finely shredded
1 fresh red chilli, seeded and
   finely chopped
60ml/4 tbsp water
5ml/1 tsp clear honey
15ml/1 tbsp Thai fish sauce
15ml/1 tbsp light soy sauce

Serves 4

NUTRITIONAL INFORMATION Energy 99kcal/410kJ; Protein 3.4g;
Carbohydrate 3.1g, of which sugars 3g; Fat 8.2g, of which saturates 1.1g;
Cholesterol 0mg; Calcium 50mg; Fibre 1.8g; Sodium 269mg

1 Snap off the woody base of the asparagus stalks and discard.

2 Heat the oil in a wok or frying pan and stir-fry the garlic, sesame seeds and galangal or ginger for 3–4 seconds, until the garlic is just beginning to turn golden, but don't let it burn.

3 Add the asparagus stalks and chilli, toss to mix, then add the water and honey. Using two spoons, toss over the heat for a further 2 minutes, or until the asparagus just begins to soften and the liquid is well reduced.

4 Sprinkle over the fish and soy sauces, toss again and serve.

WHITE CABBAGE SLAW WITH OLIVES

The saltiness of the black olives contrasts with the sweetness of the cabbage in this salad packed with nutrients. It's a great quick, prebiotic side dish for a midweek meal.

1 small white cabbage, cut in quarters, outer leaves discarded, stems and base trimmed off
12 black olives in brine, pitted

For the dressing
75–90ml/5–6 tbsp extra virgin olive oil
30ml/2 tbsp lemon juice
1 garlic clove, crushed
30ml/2 tbsp finely chopped fresh flat leaf parsley
sea salt

Serves 4

NUTRITIONAL INFORMATION Energy 307kcal/1269kJ; Protein 3.9g; Carbohydrate 12.8g, of which sugars 12.5g; Fat 26.9g, of which saturates 3.8g; Cholesterol 0mg; Calcium 145mg; Fibre 5.8g; Sodium 21mg

1 Lay each quarter of cabbage in turn on its side and cut long, very thin slices until you reach the central core, which should be discarded. The key to a perfect cabbage slaw is to shred the cabbage as finely as possible. Place the shredded cabbage in a bowl and stir in the black olives.

2 Make the dressing by whisking the olive oil, lemon juice, garlic, chopped parsley and salt to taste together.

3 Pour the dressing over the salad, and toss the cabbage and olives until everything is evenly coated. Leave to stand for 15–30 minutes to allow the flavours to develop.

SAUERKRAUT SALAD WITH CRANBERRIES PROBIOTIC

This is a great way of eating probiotic sauerkraut as the salad is packed with vitamin C and phytonutrients from the cranberries, which are also a prebiotic fruit, and with apples that help regulate your blood sugar levels and which are a good source of fibre.

500g/1¼lb sauerkraut, to make
 your own see recipe page 35
2 red apples
100–200g/3½–7oz/scant
 1–1¾ cups fresh cranberries
60–75ml/4–5 tbsp sunflower oil
30ml/2 tbsp clear honey
 (preferably orange blossom)
2–3 sprigs fresh parsley, to garnish

Serves 4

COOK'S TIP
When fresh cranberries
aren't available you can
use thawed frozen ones or,
for a change, try another
tangy fruit such as cubes of
fresh pineapple.

NUTRITIONAL INFORMATION Energy 105kcal/437kJ; Protein 1.3g;
Carbohydrate 8.8g, of which sugars 8.8g; Fat 7.4g, of which saturates 0.9g;
Cholesterol 0mg; Calcium 49mg; Fibre 3.1g; Sodium 493mg

1 Put the sauerkraut in a colander and drain thoroughly. Taste, and if you find it is too sour, rinse it under cold running water then drain well. Put the sauerkraut in a large bowl.

2 Slice or cut the apples into slices or wedges. Add the apples and the cranberries to the sauerkraut.

3 Whisk the oil and honey together, drizzle over and toss well. Serve garnished with parsley sprigs.

GRATED BEETROOT AND YOGURT SALAD PROBIOTIC

This salad is almost a dip, made with grated beetroot, probiotic yogurt and spiked with prebiotic garlic; it's a pretty shade of pink and is very moreish scooped on to toasted flatbreads or chunks of a warm, crusty sourdough bread.

4 raw beetroot (beets), washed and stalks trimmed (don't cut into the beetroot though, or it will bleed when cooked)
500ml/17fl oz/generous 2 cups live bio Greek (US strained plain) yogurt
2 garlic cloves, crushed
sea salt and black pepper
a few fresh mint leaves, shredded, to garnish

Serves 4

COOK'S TIP
Cooking fresh beetroot gives it the highest nutritional content but you could use ready-cooked vacuum-packed ones for this recipe, just not ones pickled in vinegar.

NUTRITIONAL INFORMATION Energy 95kcal/403kJ; Protein 7.8g; Carbohydrate 14.4g, of which sugars 13g; Fat 1.4g, of which saturates 0.6g; Cholesterol 2mg; Calcium 249mg; Fibre 1.3g; Sodium 137mg

1 Boil the beetroot in plenty of water for 35–40 minutes until tender, but not mushy or soft.

2 Drain the beetroot and refresh under cold running water, then peel off the skins and roughly grate the beetroot on to a plate. Squeeze it lightly in kitchen paper to drain off excess water.

3 In a bowl, beat the yogurt with the garlic and season with salt and pepper. Add the beetroot, reserving a little to garnish the top, and mix well. Garnish with mint leaves.

DESSERTS AND BAKES

The following recipes contain a lovely mix of probiotic and prebiotic ingredients for the best of both worlds, so the labels top right refer to whether they are predominantly one or the other. I've used honey instead of sugar to give maximum digestive benefits but you could use golden caster sugar instead if you prefer. Having a small slice of something nutritious mid afternoon is a good way of keeping your blood sugar levels constant and energy levels up. It will also help stave off hunger pangs so you aren't tempted to overeat in the evening.

LITTLE BLUEBERRY PIES

PREBIOTIC

These delicious little pies, made with a yeast-based pastry, are perfect as a dessert after a Sunday lunch or great for a mid-afternoon snack with a cup of tea or coffee. They look very pretty with a little sifted icing sugar dusted over, but I usually omit this.

For the pastry
50g/2oz/¼ cup butter
200ml/7fl oz/scant 1 cup milk
45ml/3 tbsp water
2.5ml/½ tsp salt
7.5ml/1½ tsp clear honey
1 small (US medium) egg
400g/14oz/3½ cups spelt flour
7.5ml/1½ tsp easy-blend (rapid-rise) dried yeast

For the filling
300–350g/11–12oz/2¾–3 cups
  blueberries, fresh or frozen
30ml/2 tbsp clear honey
15ml/1 tbsp potato flour

For the glaze
150ml/¼ pint/⅔ cup sour cream
  or crème fraîche
45ml/3 tbsp clear honey
icing (confectioners') sugar,
  for dusting (optional)

Makes 10

NUTRITIONAL INFORMATION Energy 371kcal/1559kJ; Protein 4.4g; Carbohydrate 55.8g, of which sugars 25.7g; Fat 16g, of which saturates 4.9g; Cholesterol 8mg; Calcium 93mg; Fibre 3.2g; Sodium 228mg

1 First make the pastry. Melt the butter in a small pan, add the milk, water, salt and honey and heat until warm to the fingertips. Pour the milk mixture into a large bowl. Add the egg and whisk lightly to mix. Put the flour and yeast in a large bowl and mix together. Stir in the milk and butter mixture, a little at a time, until combined.

2 Knead the dough in the bowl for at least 5 minutes. Cover the bowl with a dish towel and leave the dough to rise in a warm place for 30 minutes, until it has doubled in size. Turn the dough on to a lightly floured surface. Cut the pastry into 10 equal-size pieces and form each piece into a ball. Leave to rest for 5–10 minutes.

3 Meanwhile, prepare the filling. Put the blueberries in a bowl, add the honey and potato flour and mix together. Preheat the oven to 200°C/400°F/Gas 6. Grease a large baking tray. Flatten each pastry ball to a round measuring about 15cm/6in in diameter.

4 Place the pastry rounds on the baking tray. Place 45ml/3 tbsp of the blueberry mixture in the centre of each round, then crimp a small edge up around the mixture. Bake the pies in the oven for 10–15 minutes, until golden brown. Meanwhile, make the glaze. Put the sour cream or crème fraîche and the honey in a bowl and mix together.

5 When the pies are baked, gently spoon a little of the glaze over each pie. Dust the tops with sifted icing sugar, if using. Serve hot or cold.

TOFU BERRY CHEESECAKE

This summery dessert is a very light and refreshing finish to any meal. Strictly speaking, it is not a cheesecake at all, as it's based on tofu – but no one would guess. So indulge yourself with a slice, happy in the knowledge it's actually helping your digestion and all-round health with plenty of prebiotics and probiotics and no added sugar.

For the base
50g/2oz/4 tbsp butter
30ml/2 tbsp apple juice
115g/4oz/6 cups bran flakes or
    other high-fibre cereal

For the filling
275g/10oz/1¼ cups silken tofu,
    drained
200ml/7fl oz/scant 1 cup live
    bio yogurt
scraped seeds from 1 vanilla pod
    (bean)
15ml/1 tbsp powdered gelatine
60ml/4 tbsp apple juice

For the topping
175g/6oz/1½ cups mixed summer
    soft fruit, e.g. strawberries,
    raspberries, redcurrants,
    blackberries, etc. (or frozen
    'fruits of the forest')
30ml/2 tbsp redcurrant jelly

Serves 6

COOK'S TIP
Use a reduced-fat butter if
you prefer for the base.

NUTRITIONAL INFORMATION Energy 204kcal/854kJ; Protein 7.7g; Carbohydrate 23.2g, of which sugars 13.8g; Fat 9.5g, of which saturates 0.5g; Cholesterol 0mg; Calcium 311mg; Fibre 2.8g; Sodium 253mg

1 For the base, place the butter and apple juice in a pan and heat them gently until the butter has melted. Crush the cereal and stir it into the pan.

2 Tip into a 23cm/9in round loose-bottomed flan tin or pie pan and press down firmly. Leave to set.

3 For the filling, place the tofu, yogurt and vanilla seeds in a blender or food processor and process them until smooth.

4 Sprinkle the gelatine over the apple juice in a small bowl and leave to soften for 5 minutes. Either stand the bowl in a pan of gently simmering water and stir until the gelatine has completely dissolved or heat briefly in the microwave (but do not allow to boil) and stir until completely dissolved. Stir immediately into the tofu mixture.

5 Spread the tofu mixture over the firm base, smoothing it evenly. Chill in the refrigerator until the filling has set. Remove the flan tin and place the dessert on a serving plate.

6 Arrange the fruits over the top. Melt the redcurrant jelly with 30ml/2 tbsp hot water and spoon or brush all over the fruits to glaze. Chill in the refrigerator until the glaze has set, then serve in slices.

CHOCOLATE SORBET WITH RED FRUITS

PREBIOTIC

Isn't it great that good-quality dark chocolate is a prebiotic? However, you should never eat it in large quantities, as even very dark chocolate is loaded with fat and some sugar so won't help your waistline if you overdo it. This recipe uses a very small amount.

475ml/16fl oz/2 cups water
90ml/6 tbsp clear honey
75g/3oz/¾ cup unsweetened cocoa powder
50g/2oz dark (bittersweet) chocolate, at least 70% cocoa solids, chopped into small pieces
400g/14oz soft red fruits, such as raspberries, redcurrants and strawberries

Serves 6

NUTRITIONAL INFORMATION 301kcal/1266kJ; Protein 2.3g; Carbohydrate 48.1g, of which sugars 47.7g; Fat 12.4g, of which saturates 7.4g; Cholesterol 3mg; Calcium 25mg; Fibre 1.1g; Sodium 4mg

1 Place the water, honey, and cocoa powder in a pan. Heat gently, stirring occasionally, until well blended then bring to the boil. Remove the pan from the heat, add the chocolate and stir until melted. Leave until cold.

2 Tip into an ice cream maker and churn until frozen. Alternatively, pour into a container suitable for use in the freezer, freeze until slushy, whisk until smooth, then freeze again. Whisk for a second time before the mixture hardens completely, and cover the container.

3 Remove from the freezer 10–15 minutes before serving, so that the sorbet softens slightly. Serve in scoops in chilled dessert bowls, with the soft fruits.

STRAWBERRY MOUSSE

This is a gloriously fresh-tasting mousse with honey instead of sugar and crème fraîche instead of thick cream for great probiotics. Use half raspberries and half strawberries if you prefer to add a little tartness and a good mix of prebiotics too.

250g/9oz strawberries, hulled
90ml/6 tbsp clear honey
75ml/2½fl oz/⅓ cup white wine
75ml/2½fl oz/⅓ cup cold water
15ml/1 tbsp powdered gelatine
60ml/4 tbsp boiling water
300ml/½ pint/1¼ cups crème fraîche
fresh mint leaves, to decorate

Serves 4

NUTRITIONAL INFORMATION Energy 441kcal/1835kJ; Protein 18.1g; Carbohydrate 22.9g, of which sugars 22.6g; Fat 30.1g, of which saturates 20.3g; Cholesterol 85mg; Calcium 103mg; Fibre 0.9g; Sodium 85mg

1 Chop most of the strawberries, reserving a few whole ones for decoration. Blend the chopped strawberries in a food processor with the honey and wine to a smooth purée.

2 Put the cold water in a large bowl and sprinkle over the gelatine. Leave to soften for 5 minutes, then add the boiling water and stir until the gelatine has completely dissolved.

3 Mix the strawberry mixture with the dissolved gelatine. Chill for about 30 minutes, or until the mixture is starting to thicken.

4 Lightly whip the crème fraîche until soft peaks form, then gently fold into the thickened strawberry mixture. Spoon the mousse into glasses and chill overnight in the refrigerator. Decorate with a strawberry and mint leaves and serve.

COFFEE BANANAS

Rich, lavish and sinful-looking, this dessert takes only about two minutes to make and is far from bad for you – it's positively health-giving with prebiotic bananas and honey and probiotic yogurt and a sprinkling of magnesium-rich almonds.

4 small ripe bananas
a squeeze of lemon juice
15ml/1 tbsp instant coffee
   granules or powder
30ml/2 tbsp clear honey
250ml/8fl oz/1 cup live bio Greek
   (US strained plain) yogurt
15ml/1 tbsp toasted flaked
   (sliced) almonds

Serves 4

COOK'S TIP
For a special occasion, add
a dash of dark rum or
brandy to the bananas for
extra richness.

NUTRITIONAL INFORMATION Energy 186kcal/782kJ; Protein 5g;
Carbohydrate 29.5g, of which sugars 27.3g; Fat 6.1g, of which saturates
2.9g; Cholesterol 9mg; Calcium 110mg; Fibre 1.3g; Sodium 97mg

1 Peel and slice one banana and toss in the lemon juice. Mash the remaining three bananas with a fork.

2 Dissolve the coffee in 15ml/1 tbsp of hot water and stir in the honey. Mix into the mashed bananas.

3 Spoon a little of the mashed banana mixture into four serving dishes. Top with a spoonful of yogurt, then repeat until all the ingredients are used up, ending with a layer of yogurt.

4 Swirl the last layer of yogurt for a marbled effect. Finish with a few banana slices and flaked almonds. Serve cold. Best eaten within about an hour of making.

DATE AND TOFU ICE

Dates and carminative cinnamon pack this smooth probiotic ice with flavour. This is another dessert that delivers mouthfuls of goodness to really help your gut flora balance. Soya milk boosts the probiotic content but you could use cow's milk instead.

250g/9oz/1½ cups stoned
   (pitted) dates
600ml/1 pint/2½ cups apple juice
5ml/1 tsp ground cinnamon
285g/10oz tofu, drained and cubed
150ml/¼ pint/⅔ cup unsweetened
   soya milk

Serves 6

COOK'S TIP
This is particularly good served sprinkled with some passion fruit pulp or with some sliced bananas or a mixture of banana and fresh pineapple or canned pineapple in natural juice.

....
NUTRITIONAL INFORMATION Energy 290kcal/1232kJ; Protein 9.1g;
Carbohydrate 58.2g, of which sugars 57.9g; Fat 3.9g, of which saturates
0.5g; Cholesterol 0mg; Calcium 407mg; Fibre 2.5g; Sodium 24mg
....

1 Put the dates in a pan. Pour in 300ml/½ pint/1¼ cups of the apple juice and leave to soak for 2 hours. Simmer for 10 minutes, then leave to cool. Using a slotted spoon, lift out one-quarter of the dates, chop roughly and set aside.

2 Purée the remaining dates in a blender or food processor. Add the cinnamon and enough of the remaining apple juice to process to a smooth paste. Add the cubes of tofu to the food processor, a few at a time, processing after each addition. Add the remaining apple juice and the soya milk and mix well.

3 Spoon the blended mixture into a freezerproof container and freeze for 2–3 hours until firm around the edges. Whisk to break up the ice crystals then freeze again for 2 hours. Whisk again, stir in the dates reserving a few for decoration, and then freeze until firm. Serve in glasses, topped with chopped dates.

BLUEBERRY HONEY ICE CREAM PARFAIT

This light and luscious frozen dessert is packed with prebiotic blueberries and honey but mixed with probiotic crème fraîche for a perfect combination. I've used grated lemon zest but lime zest goes equally well to bring out the flavour of the blueberries.

2 large (US extra large) eggs,
  separated
115g/4oz/½ cup light clear honey
200g/7oz/1¾ cups blueberries
finely grated zest of ½ lemon
300ml/½ pint/1¼ cups crème
  fraîche

Serves 4

COOK'S TIP
This basic recipe can be used with different flavourings, such as the grated rind of 1 orange or 30ml/2 tbsp chopped crystallized stem ginger or 30ml/2 tbsp raisins and 30ml/2 tbsp rum.

NUTRITIONAL INFORMATION Energy 452kcal/1875kJ; Protein 6.5g; Carbohydrate 31.3g, of which sugars 28.8g; Fat 34.4g, of which saturates 21.5g; Cholesterol 229mg; Calcium 66mg; Fibre 1.6g; Sodium 73mg

1 Put the egg yolks and half the honey in a bowl and whisk together until pale and thick.

2 Beat in about three-quarters of the blueberries and reserve the remainder for decorating. Blend in the berries so that some burst slightly and spread their colour. Stir in the lemon zest.

3 Whisk the egg whites until they form soft peaks. Whisk in the remaining honey.

4 Whisk the crème fraîche until it just holds its shape, and fold into the blueberry mixture then fold in the egg white mixture.

5 Transfer to a mould or freezer container and freeze for 6–8 hours until firm, or churn in an ice cream maker, then store in a sealed container in the freezer.

6 Unless the berries were very juicy, it should be possible to serve the ice cream parfait straight from the freezer. However, if the berries produced a lot of juice, it is better to put the parfait in the refrigerator for about 20 minutes to allow it to soften slightly before being served.

7 To serve, if using a mould, dip it briefly in hot water before turning out on to a serving platter. Alternatively, serve in scoops and decorate with the reserved blueberries.

HONEY AND ALMOND COOKIES

These delectable spiced honey cookies keep well stored in an airtight container and are full of prebiotic honey and spelt flour along with wonderful carminative spices.

225g/8oz/1 cup clear honey
4 eggs, plus 2 egg whites, beaten
350g/12oz/3 cups spelt flour
5ml/1 tsp bicarbonate of soda
  (baking soda)
2.5ml/½ tsp freshly grated nutmeg
2.5ml/½ tsp ground ginger
2.5ml/½ tsp ground cinnamon
2.5ml/½ tsp ground cloves
20 blanched almonds

Makes 20

COOK'S TIP
The leftover egg yolks will keep in the refrigerator, covered, for up to 2 days.

NUTRITIONAL INFORMATION Per cookie: Energy 112kcal/473kJ; Protein 3.4g; Carbohydrate 22.6g, of which sugars 8.9g; Fat 1.5g, of which saturates 0.4g; Cholesterol 38mg; Calcium 33mg; Fibre 0.5g; Sodium 22mg

1 Beat together the honey and whole eggs until light and fluffy. Sift over the flour, bicarbonate of soda and spices, and beat to combine. Gather into a ball, wrap in plastic wrap and chill in the refrigerator for 1 hour. Preheat the oven to 200°C/400°F/Gas 6.

2 Roll out the dough on a lightly floured surface to a thickness of 5mm/¼in. With a 4cm/1½in cookie cutter, stamp out 20 rounds. Transfer to 2 lightly greased baking sheets.

3 Brush the tops of the rounds with the beaten egg white, then press an almond on top. Bake for 15–20 minutes, or until they are a pale golden brown. Remove from the oven and allow to cool slightly before transferring to a wire cooling rack.

FRUITY MUESLI BARS

These fruity flapjacks make an appetizing, high-fibre and nourishing treat for a portable snack and will keep hunger pangs at bay while boosting your digestion with the prebiotic oats.

115g/4oz/½ cup butter, plus extra
   for greasing
105ml/7 tbsp clear honey
150g/5oz/1¼ cups no-added sugar
   Swiss-style muesli (granola)
50g/2oz/½ cup rolled oats
5ml/1 tsp ground mixed (apple
   pie) spice
50g/2oz/⅓ cup sultanas
   (golden raisins)
50g/2oz/⅓ cup ready-to-eat dried
   pears or apricots, chopped

Makes 10–12

NUTRITIONAL INFORMATION Energy 178kcal/744kJ; Protein 2.2g; Carbohydrate 22.7g, of which sugars 13.2g; Fat 9.3g, of which saturates 5.2g; Cholesterol 20mg; Calcium 16mg; Fibre 2.1g; Sodium 68mg

1 Preheat the oven to 180°C/350°F/Gas 4. Lightly grease an 18cm/7in square cake tin or pan. Put the butter and honey in a pan and gently heat, stirring until melted and blended.

2 Remove the pan from the heat, and add the muesli, rolled oats, mixed spice, sultanas and chopped pears or apricots. Stir with a wooden spoon to mix thoroughly.

3 Transfer the mixture to the prepared cake tin and level the surface, pressing down firmly with the back of a spoon.

4 Bake for 20–30 minutes, until golden brown. Cool for a few minutes in the tin, then mark into 10 to 12 squares using a sharp knife. Leave to cool and firm up in the tin, then, when almost cold, cut into bars and leave on a wire rack until completely cold before storing in an airtight container.

BANANA BREAD

This is the ideal way to use up over-ripe bananas. Another good option is to pop them into smoothies. The prebiotic-packed bananas for this recipe must be very ripe as they give the sweetness to the bread. If they are not quite ripe enough, add 15ml/1tbsp clear honey to the mixture. You can use any milk for this such as soya, almond or oat milk but I always use semi-skimmed cow's milk for maximum calcium.

115g/4oz/½ cup butter, softened,
    plus extra for greasing
5ml/1 tsp bicarbonate of soda
    (baking soda)
225g/8oz/2 cups wholemeal
    (whole-wheat) flour
2 eggs, beaten
3 very ripe bananas
30–45ml/2–3 tbsp milk

Serves 10–12

COOK'S TIP
To add a little spice to the cake, add 5ml/1 tsp ground cinnamon to the mixture. Sunflower or pumpkin seeds or chopped walnuts make a good addition too. Add about 50g/2oz/ ½ cup to the mixture just before baking.

NUTRITIONAL INFORMATION Energy 169kcal/709kJ; Protein 4.1g; Carbohydrate 18g, of which sugars 5.8g; Fat 9.5g, of which saturates 5.4g; Cholesterol 59mg; Calcium 19mg; Fibre 2.6g; Sodium 188mg

1 Preheat the oven to 180°C/350°F/Gas 4. Grease and base line a 23 x 13cm/9 x 5in loaf tin or pan.

2 Cream the butter in a bowl until it is fluffy. Sift the bicarbonate of soda with the flour, then gradually add to the creamed butter, alternately with the eggs.

3 Peel the bananas and slice them into a bowl. Mash them well, then stir them into the cake mixture. Mix in enough milk to create a dropping consistency.

4 Spoon the mixture into the loaf tin and level the surface with a spoon.

5 Bake for about 1¼ hours or until a fine skewer inserted in the centre comes out clean. Cool on a wire rack. Serve in slices, as it is or spread with butter.

SAN FRANCISCO SOURDOUGH

Sourdough is leavened using a flour and water paste, which is left to ferment with airborne yeast. The finished loaf has a moist crumb and crispy crust, and will keep well. Don't be daunted by the number of steps as each little bit doesn't take long, and if you get into the habit of creating your own probiotic bread, your gut will be so much healthier.

For the starter
50g/2oz/½ cup wholemeal
   (whole-wheat) flour
pinch of ground cumin
15ml/1 tbsp milk
15–30ml/1–2 tbsp water

For the first starter refreshment
30ml/2 tbsp water
115g/4oz/1 cup wholemeal
   (whole-wheat) flour

For the second starter
   refreshment
60ml/4 tbsp water
115g/4oz/1 cup unbleached white
   bread flour

For the first bread refreshment
75ml/5 tbsp very warm water
75g/3oz/¾ cup unbleached plain
   (all-purpose) flour

For the second bread
   refreshment
175ml/6fl oz/¾ cup lukewarm
   water
200–225g/7–8oz/1¾–2 cups
   unbleached plain
   (all-purpose) flour

For the bread
280ml/9fl oz/1¼ cups warm water
500g/1¼lb/5 cups unbleached
   white bread flour
15ml/1 tbsp salt
flour, for dusting
ice cubes, for baking

Makes 2 medium loaves

NUTRITIONAL INFORMATION per slice (¹⁄₁₂ loaf) Energy 146kcal/619.6kJ; Protein 4g; Carbohydrate 33.2g, of which sugars 0.6g; Fat 0.6g, of which saturates 0.1g; Cholesterol 0mg; Calcium 60mg; Fibre 1.3g; Sodium 124mg

1 For the starter, sift the wholemeal flour and cumin into a bowl. Add the milk and sufficient water to make a moist but not sticky, dough. Knead for 6–8 minutes to form a firm dough.

2 Return the dough to the bowl, cover with a damp dish towel and leave in a warm place, 24–26°C/75–80°F, for about 2 days. When it is ready the starter will appear moist and wrinkled and will have developed a crust.

3 Pull off the hardened crust and discard. Scoop out the moist centre (about the size of a hazelnut), which will be aerated and sweet-smelling, and place in a clean bowl. Mix in the water for the first starter refreshment. Gradually add the wholemeal flour and mix to a dough.

4 Cover with clear film or plastic wrap and leave in a warm place for 1–2 days. Discard the crust and gradually mix in the water for the second starter refreshment, which by now will have a slightly sharper smell. Gradually mix in the white bread flour, cover and leave in a warm place for 8–10 hours.

5 For the first bread refreshment, mix the starter with the water. Gradually mix in the plain flour to form a firm dough. Knead for 6–8 minutes until smooth and firm. Cover with a damp dish towel and leave in a warm place for 8–12 hours, or until doubled in bulk.

6 Gradually mix in the water for the second bread refreshment, then mix in enough plain flour to form a soft, smooth elastic dough. Cover and leave in a warm place for 8–12 hours.

7 Gradually stir in the water for the bread, then work in the white bread flour and salt. This will take 10–15 minutes. Turn out on to a lightly floured surface and knead until smooth and elastic.

8 Place in a large lightly oiled bowl, cover with lightly oiled clear film and leave to rise, in a warm place, for 8–12 hours.

9 Divide the dough in half and shape into two round loaves by folding the sides over to the centre and sealing. Place seam sides up in flour-dusted couronnes, or baskets lined with flour-dusted dish towels. Cover and rise in a warm place for 4 hours.

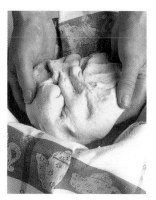

10 Preheat the oven to 220°C/425°F/Gas 7. Place an empty roasting pan in the bottom of the oven. Dust two baking sheets with flour. Turn out the loaves, seam sides down, on the prepared baking sheets. Slash a criss-cross pattern on the top of the loaves four or five times in each direction with a sharp knife.

11 Place the baking sheets in the oven and immediately drop the ice cubes into the hot roasting pan to create steam. Bake the bread for 25 minutes, then reduce the oven temperature to 200°C/400°F/Gas 6 and bake for a further 15–20 minutes, until they sound hollow when tapped on the bases. Cool on wire racks.

SOURDOUGH RYE BREAD

PROBIOTIC

This bread has healthy probiotic gut benefits of being a sourdough, together with the additional goodness of rye and wholemeal flour for extra fibre. This dark rye bread is also enriched with dark molasses, which gives a lovely flavour. Do make sure you use natural molasses free from additives.

For the starter
15ml/1 tbsp active dried yeast
350ml/12fl oz/1½ cups lukewarm
    water
45ml/3 tbsp natural black molasses
30ml/2 tbsp caraway seeds
250g/9oz/2¼ cups rye flour

For the bread
10ml/2 tsp active dried yeast
120ml/4fl oz/½ cup lukewarm
    water
25g/1oz/2 tbsp butter, melted
15ml/1 tbsp salt
115g/4oz/1 cup strong wholemeal
    (whole-wheat) bread flour
400–450g/14–16oz/3½–4 cups
    unbleached strong white
    bread flour
1 egg mixed with 15ml/1 tbsp
    water, for glazing

Makes 2 loaves

NUTRITIONAL INFORMATION per slice (1/12 loaf) Energy 189kcal/799kJ; Protein 6.8g; Carbohydrate 38.6g, of which sugars 0.9g; Fat 1.4g, of which saturates 0.1g; Cholesterol 0mg; Calcium 18mg; Fibre 4.6g; Sodium 1mg

1 For the starter, combine the yeast and water, stir and leave for 15 minutes to dissolve.

2 Stir in the molasses, caraway seeds and rye flour. Cover and leave in a warm place for 2–3 days to ferment.

3 When the starter is ready, you can make the bread. In a large bowl, combine the yeast and water, stir and leave for 10 minutes. Stir in the melted butter, salt, wholemeal flour and 400g/14oz/3½ cups of the white bread flour.

4 Make a well in the centre and pour in the starter. Mix to a rough dough, then transfer to a floured surface and knead for several minutes until smooth and elastic. Return to the bowl, cover and leave to rise in a warm place until doubled in volume, about 2 hours.

5 Grease a large baking sheet. Knock back or punch down the dough and knead briefly. Cut the dough in half and form each half into a log-shaped loaf.

6 Place the loaves on the baking sheet and score the tops with a sharp knife. Cover and leave to rise in a warm place until almost doubled, about 50 minutes.

7 Preheat the oven to 190°C/375°F/Gas 5. Brush the loaves with the beaten egg mixed with water to glaze them, then bake for 50–55 minutes, until the bottoms sound hollow when tapped. If browning too quickly, lay a sheet of foil loosely over the tops to protect them. Cool on a wire rack.

PUMPERNICKEL

This famous German bread is extremely dense and dark, with an intense flavour. It is simpler than most sourdough loaves as it needs no starter and is an excellent probiotic.

450g/1lb/4 cups rye flour
225g/8oz/2 cups wholemeal (whole-wheat) flour
115g/4oz/²⁄₃ cup bulgur wheat
10ml/2 tsp sea salt
30ml/2 tbsp molasses
600ml/1 pint/2½ cups cups warm water
15ml/1 tbsp vegetable oil

Makes 2 loaves

COOK'S TIP
This bread improves on keeping. Keep for at least 24 hours double-wrapped in baking parchment and then foil before serving.

NUTRITIONAL INFORMATION (per slice) Energy 116kcal/493kJ; Protein 3.2g; Carbohydrate 24.7g, of which sugars 1g; Fat 1.1g, of which saturates 0.1g; Cholesterol 0mg; Calcium 19mg; Fibre 4.1g; Sodium 167mg

1 Lightly grease two 18 × 9cm/7 × 3½in loaf tins or pans. Mix the rye flour, wholemeal flour, bulgur wheat and salt together in a large bowl. Mix the molasses with the warm water and add to the flours with the vegetable oil to form a dense mass.

2 Place in the prepared tins, pressing into the corners. Cover with lightly oiled clear film or plastic wrap and leave in a warm place for 18–24 hours. Preheat the oven to 110°C/225°F/Gas ¼.

3 Cover the loaf tins tightly with foil. Fill a roasting pan with boiling water and place the tins on a rack inside the pan. Bake for 4 hours.

4 Increase the oven temperature to 160°C/325°F/Gas 3. Top up the water if necessary, uncover the loaves and bake for 30–45 minutes more, until the tops are crusty.

WHOLEMEAL SCONES

These make a great alternative to bread for breakfast. For a good-for-your-gut treat, top with a dollop of crème fraîche to add some probiotics, and a spoonful of blueberry jam.

350g/12oz/3 cups wholemeal (whole-wheat) flour
150g/5oz/1¼ cups unbleached plain (all-purpose) flour
2.5ml/½ tsp salt
12.5ml/2½ tsp bicarbonate of soda (baking soda)
175g/6oz/¾ cup cold butter, diced, plus extra for greasing
2 eggs
30ml/2 tbsp honey
175ml/6fl oz/¾ cup buttermilk

Makes about 16

VARIATION
Add 30ml/2 tbsp raisins to the dry mixture in step 2, if you wish. You can also make cheese scones by adding 50g/2oz grated Cheddar at the same stage.

NUTRITIONAL INFORMATION Energy 245kcal/1027kJ; Protein 6.2g; Carbohydrate 33g, of which sugars 2.8g; Fat 10.7g, of which saturates 6.1g; Cholesterol 52mg; Calcium 58mg; Fibre 3.5g; Sodium 360mg

1 Preheat the oven to 200°C/400°F/Gas 6. Grease and flour a large baking sheet.

2 Combine the dry ingredients in a bowl. Add the butter and rub in with your fingertips until the mixture resembles coarse breadcrumbs. Set aside.

3 In another bowl, whisk together the eggs, honey and buttermilk. Set aside 30ml/2 tbsp for glazing. Stir the remaining egg mixture into the dry ingredients until it holds together.

4 Roll or pat out the dough to about 2cm/¾in thick. Stamp out circles with a biscuit or cookie cutter. Place on the prepared sheet and brush with the glaze. Bake for 12–15 minutes until golden. Allow to cool slightly before serving warm.

WHOLEMEAL SUNFLOWER BREAD

PREBIOTIC

Adding seeds to bread is a wonderful way of making it more nutritious and interesting. Sunflower seeds give a nutty crunchiness to this high-fibre, prebiotic wholemeal loaf, which tastes delicious served simply with a chunk of good aged cheese and, perhaps some prebiotic tomato chutney (see Cook's Tip below).

450g/1lb/4 cups wholemeal
  (whole-wheat) flour
2.5ml/½ tsp easy-blend (rapid-rise)
  dried yeast
2.5ml/½ tsp salt
50g/2oz/½ cup sunflower seeds,
  plus extra for sprinkling
10ml/2 tsp clear honey
300ml/½ pint/1¼ cups warm
  water

Makes 1 loaf

COOK'S TIP
To make a quick prebiotic tomato chutney, skin and chop 6 ripe tomatoes. Place in a pan with 1 chopped shallot, a pinch of mixed (apple pie) spice and mixed herbs, 15ml/1 tbsp clear honey and a splash of white wine vinegar. Simmer until pulpy, then season to taste and leave to cool. Store in a sterilized screw-topped jar in the refrigerator and use within 2 weeks.

NUTRITIONAL INFORMATION (per slice) Energy 143kcal/605kJ; Protein 5.6g; Carbohydrate 25.4g, of which sugars 1.5g; Fat 2.8g, of which saturates 0.4g; Cholesterol 0mg; Calcium 19mg; Fibre 4.8g; Sodium 83mg

1 Grease and lightly flour a 450g/1lb loaf tin or pan. Mix together the flour, yeast, salt and sunflower seeds in a large bowl. Stir the honey into the warm water. Make a well in the centre of the flour mixture and gradually stir in. Mix vigorously with a wooden spoon to form a soft, sticky dough.

2 Cover the bowl with a damp dish towel and leave the dough to rise in a warm place for 45–50 minutes, or until doubled in bulk.

3 Preheat the oven to 200°C/400°F/Gas 6. Turn out the dough on to a floured work surface and knead for 10 minutes – it will still be quite sticky.

4 Form the dough into a rectangle and put in the prepared tin. Sprinkle the sunflower seeds over the top. Cover with a damp dish towel and leave to rise for 15 minutes.

5 Bake for 40–45 minutes, until golden and firm to the touch. Leave for 5 minutes, then turn out of the tin, tap the base to check it sounds hollow and leave to cool on a wire rack.

DRINKS

A glass of something delicious and healthy is a great way of getting your probiotics and prebiotics in a hurry. If you are not a breakfast person, in particular, some of the smoothies are a good way to gulp down goodness before you embark on your day. Many of these drinks are ideal for getting kids to consume more fruit and vegetables without really knowing it, and they are all much better options than the sugar-sweetened ones you buy in bottles. There is also an aromatic recipe for spiced tea, or chai, along with the most indulgent hot chocolate ever.

MANGO AND LIME LASSI

PROBIOTIC

This tangy, fruity blend is great for breakfast or as a pick-me-up at any time of day. Soft, ripe mango blended with probiotic yogurt and sharp, zesty lime and lemon juice makes a wonderfully thick, cooling drink that's packed with energy.

1 mango
finely grated zest and juice of
  1 lime
15ml/1 tbsp lemon juice
5–10ml/1–2 tsp clear honey, or
  to taste
100ml/3½fl oz/scant ½ cup live
  bio yogurt
iced water
1 extra lime, halved, to serve

Makes 2 glasses

NUTRITIONAL INFORMATION Energy 81kcal/344kJ; Protein 3.1g; Carbohydrate 17g, of which sugars 16.7g; Fat 0.7g, of which saturates 0.4g; Cholesterol 1mg; Calcium 106mg; Fibre 2g; Sodium 43mg

1 Peel the mango and cut the flesh from the stone or pit. Put the flesh into a food processor or blender and add the lime zest and juice. Add the lemon juice, honey and natural yogurt.

2 Whizz until completely smooth, scraping down the sides once or twice. Thin down with iced water, stirring well, to create a drinkable consistency.

3 Serve immediately, with half a lime on the side of each glass so that more juice can be squeezed in if desired.

ZESTY SOYA SMOOTHIE

Whizzed up with freshly squeezed orange juice, a splash of lemon and a little fragrant honey, tofu is transformed into a stunning probiotic drink that's smooth, creamy, and packed with protein, calcium and vitamin C.

2 oranges
15ml/1 tbsp lemon juice
20–25ml/4–5 tsp sunflower or
   herb honey (I love thyme honey)
150g/5oz tofu

Makes 1 glass

NUTRITIONAL INFORMATION Energy 350kcal/1483kJ; Protein 15.6g; Carbohydrate 60.9g, of which sugars 60.3g; Fat 6.6g, of which saturates 0.8g; Cholesterol 0mg; Calcium 908mg; Fibre 5.1g; Sodium 26mg

1 Finely grate the zest from the oranges and place in a blender or food processor. Squeeze the orange juice and add to the zest with the lemon juice, honey and tofu.

2 Whizz the ingredients until very smooth and creamy and serve in a tall glass, decorated with strips of orange zest, if you like.

STRAWBERRY AND TOFU SMOOTHIE

This energizing blend is simply bursting with probiotic and prebiotic goodness and inside one glass you will be getting a hit of calcium, vitamins, minerals, protein and soluble fibre too. This is another quick and easy breakfast blend.

200g/7oz/1¾ cups strawberries,
   hulled and roughly chopped
250g/9oz silken tofu,
   roughly chopped
45ml/3 tbsp pumpkin or sunflower
   seeds, plus extra for sprinkling
15–30ml/1–2 tbsp clear honey
juice of 2 large oranges
juice of 1 lemon

Makes 2 glasses

NUTRITIONAL INFORMATION Energy 289kcal/1204kJ; Protein 15.7g; Carbohydrate 21.2g, of which sugars 16.9g; Fat 16.1g, of which saturates 1.7g; Cholesterol 0mg; Calcium 684mg; Fibre 2.5g; Sodium 18mg

1 Set aside a few strawberry chunks to garnish, then put the remaining strawberries in a blender or food processor and pulse briefly to break up.

2 Add the chopped tofu, pumpkin or sunflower seeds, honey and fruit juices to the food processor and blend until completely smooth and creamy, scraping the mixture down from the side of the bowl with a spatula, if necessary.

3 Pour the smoothie into tumblers and sprinkle the top with a few extra seeds and strawberry chunks.

ORANGE AND AVOCADO JUICE

Prebiotic asparagus is blended here with life's most nutritious fruit – the avocado – which is packed with protein, monosaturated fats and vital vitamins and minerals. Orange juice adds vitamin C for a mega health-boosting drink.

1 small avocado
small handful of parsley
75g/3oz tender asparagus spears
2 large oranges
squeeze of lemon juice
ice cubes
mineral water
orange wedges, to decorate

Makes 2 glasses

NUTRITIONAL INFORMATION Energy 123kcal/507kJ; Protein 2.3g; Carbohydrate 6.1g, of which sugars 5.4g; Fat 10g, of which saturates 2.1g; Cholesterol 0mg; Calcium 21mg; Fibre 2.4g; Sodium 9mg

1 Halve the avocado and discard the stone or pit. Scoop the flesh into a blender or food processor. Remove any tough stalks from the parsley and add.

2 Roughly chop the asparagus and add to the avocado. Blend thoroughly until smooth, scraping the mixture down from the side of the bowl, if necessary.

3 Juice the oranges and add to the mixture with the lemon juice. Blend briefly until the mixture is very smooth. Pour into two glasses until two-thirds full, then add ice cubes and mineral water. Decorate with chunky orange wedges.

BLUEBERRY HAZE

Thick, dark purple blueberry purée swirled into pale and creamy vanilla-flavoured buttermilk looks stunning, tastes divine, is packed with probiotics and prebiotics and is a fantastic home-made alternative to fruit milkshakes.

250g/9oz/2¼ cups blueberries
30ml/2 tbsp clear honey,
   or to taste
15ml/1 tbsp lemon juice
300ml/½ pint/1¼ cups buttermilk
1 vanilla pod (bean), seeds scraped
150ml/¼ pint/⅔ cup milk

Makes 2 glasses

NUTRITIONAL INFORMATION Energy 274kcal/1157kJ; Protein 9.1g; Carbohydrate 54.2g, of which sugars 49.2g; Fat 3.9g, of which saturates 2.4g; Cholesterol 13mg; Calcium 284mg; Fibre 2.5g; Sodium 99mg

1 Process the blueberries, 15ml/1 tbsp of the honey and the lemon juice in a blender until as smooth as possible. Divide between two glasses.

2 Put the buttermilk, vanilla seeds, milk and remaining honey in the blender and process until really frothy. Alternatively use a hand-held electric whisk.

3 Pour the buttermilk mixture over the blueberry purée, so the mixtures swirl together, and serve immediately.

RED DEFENDER

Boost your body's defences with this delicious blend of red fruits. Ripe, fragrant prebiotic strawberries, which are also packed with vitamin C, are blended with sweet, refreshing watermelon. The seeds, like all other seeds, are rich in essential nutrients.

200g/7oz/1¾ cups strawberries
small bunch red grapes, about
   90g/3½oz
1 small wedge of watermelon

Makes 2 glasses

NUTRITIONAL INFORMATION Energy 85kcal/362kJ; Protein 1.5g; Carbohydrate 20.1g, of which sugars 20.1g; Fat 0.5g, of which saturates 0.1g; Cholesterol 0mg; Calcium 29mg; Fibre 1.5g; Sodium 9mg

1 Hull the strawberries and halve them if they are large. Pull the grapes from their stalks. Cut away the skin from the watermelon.

2 Put the watermelon in a blender or food processor and blend until the seeds are broken up. Add the strawberries and grapes and blend until completely smooth, scraping the mixture down from the side of the bowl, if necessary.

CRANBERRY JUICE

Home-made sweet and sour cranberry juice is a fantastic prebiotic particularly if you use honey instead of sugar to sweeten it as here. Use a lovely floral honey, such as orange blossom, if you can, since it will add another level of flavour to the drink.

500g/1¼lb/5 cups fresh or
    frozen cranberries
1 litre/1¾ pints/4 cups
75ml/5 tbsp clear honey, or
    to taste
ice, to serve

Makes 4 glasses

VARIATION
Substitute lingonberries for the cranberries, if you wish, as they are also full of antioxidants, and their slightly bitter taste is softened by the sweetness of the honey.

NUTRITIONAL INFORMATION Energy 143kcal/615kJ; Protein 0.4g; Carbohydrate 37.1g, of which sugars 37.1g; Fat 0.4g, of which saturates 0g; Cholesterol 0mg; Calcium 26mg; Fibre 0g; Sodium 8mg

1 Put the cranberries in a food processor and blend until smooth. Strain the juice into a bowl, reserving the cranberries. Cover the bowl with clear film or plastic wrap and put in the refrigerator.

2 Put the reserved strained berries in a pan, add the water and bring to the boil. Reduce the heat and simmer for 5 minutes. Strain the berries through a sieve or strainer and discard them, but reserve the juice.

3 Pour the hot cranberry juice back into the pan away from the heat. Stir in the honey. Leave to cool.

4 When cool, mix the juice in the pan with the cold juice from the refrigerator. Taste and add more honey if necessary.

5 Return to the refrigerator for 2–3 hours before pouring into a decanter, jug or pitcher and keep cool until serving time. Serve in tall glasses with ice.

GAZPACHO JUICE

Inspired by the classic Spanish soup, this fabulous juice looks and tastes delicious and is packed with prebiotic tomatoes, celery and spring onion, along with carminative coriander. This is almost a meal in a glass, whizzed up in moments.

½ fresh red chilli
800g/1¾lb tomatoes, skinned
½ cucumber, roughly sliced
1 red (bell) pepper, seeded and cut
  into chunks
1 celery stick, chopped
1 spring onion (scallion),
  roughly chopped
a small handful of fresh coriander
  (cilantro), plus extra to decorate
juice of 1 lime
salt
ice cubes

Makes 4–5 glasses

NUTRITIONAL INFORMATION Energy 32kcal/137kJ; Protein 1.5g; Carbohydrate 5.7g, of which sugars 5.6g; Fat 0.5g, of which saturates 0.2g; Cholesterol 0mg; Calcium 22mg; Fibre 1.9g; Sodium 19mg

1 Using a sharp knife, seed the chilli. Add to a blender or food processor with the tomatoes, cucumber, red pepper, celery, spring onion and fresh coriander.

2 Blend well until smooth, scraping the vegetable mixture down from the side of the bowl, if necessary.

3 Add the lime juice and a pinch of salt and blend. Pour into glasses. Add ice cubes and a few coriander leaves to serve.

BROCCOLI BOOSTER

Apart from being a wonderful prebiotic, broccoli is packed with vitamins and antioxidants and contains almost as much calcium as milk. Here it's mixed with apple and lemon juice to tone down its rather strong flavour.

125g/4¼oz broccoli florets
2 eating apples
15ml/1 tbsp lemon juice
60ml/4 tbsp apple juice
ice cubes, to serve

Makes 1 glass

COOK'S TIP
This is best made with a high-speed blender. If you haven't got one, blanch the florets in boiling water for 2 minutes to soften, then drain and refresh with cold water briefly or use thawed frozen broccoli. You can also peel the apple but you will lose the insoluble fibre from the skin if you do.

NUTRITIONAL INFORMATION Energy 111kcal/475kJ; Protein 6.1g; Carbohydrate 20.1g, of which sugars 19.7g; Fat 1.3g, of which saturates 0.3g; Cholesterol 0mg; Calcium 78mg; Fibre 6.5g; Sodium 14mg

1 Cut off the thick stalks and peel the broccoli to remove the tough outer skin. Roughly chop the florets. Core and chop the apples.

2 Put all the ingredients except the ice cubes in a high-speed blender and process until smooth. Pour over ice cubes in a tall glass and serve.

BASIL BLUSH

Some herbs just don't juice well, losing their aromatic flavour and turning muddy and dull. Basil, however, is an excellent juicer, keeping its distinctive fresh fragrance and carminative properties. It's the perfect partner to prebiotic tomatoes in this vitality drink.

½ cucumber, peeled
a handful of fresh basil, plus extra
    to decorate
350g/12oz tomatoes
ice cubes

Makes 1–2 glasses

NUTRITIONAL INFORMATION Energy 40kcal/168kJ; Protein 1.9g; Carbohydrate 7g, of which sugars 6.8g; Fat 0.7g, of which saturates 0.2g; Cholesterol 0mg; Calcium 31mg; Fibre 2.4g; Sodium 19mg

1 Quarter the cucumber lengthways – do not remove the seeds. Push it through a juicer with the basil, then do the same with the tomatoes.

2 Pour the blended tomato, basil and cucumber juice over cubes of ice in one or two glasses and serve decorated with a few fresh sprigs of basil.

SOOTHING SPICED HOT CHOCOLATE

PREBIOTIC

This sensational drink is spiced with carminative cinnamon and cardamom together with probiotic vanilla for the perfect calming beverage. It is vital that the chocolate is good quality, with a high percentage of cocoa solids for the drink to have prebiotic effects.

450ml/¾ pint/2 cups milk
1 cardamom pod, bruised
1 cinnamon stick
½ vanilla pod (bean)
100g/3½oz plain (semisweet) chocolate, at least 70% cocoa solids, broken into pieces

Serves 2

NUTRITIONAL INFORMATION Energy 359kcal/1505kJ; Protein 10g; Carbohydrate 42.8g, of which sugars 42.4g; Fat 17.6g, of which saturates 10.9g; Cholesterol 19mg; Calcium 264mg; Fibre 1.7g; Sodium 116mg

1 Put the milk in a pan with the cardamom pod, cinnamon and vanilla pod, and bring to the boil. Add the chocolate and whisk until melted.

2 Strain the hot chocolate into warmed, heatproof glasses, mugs or cups and serve straight away.

CHAI TEA

Based on an Indian speciality, here warming carminative spices are infused with tea to make a soothing and milky drink sweetened with prebiotic honey.

450ml/16fl oz/scant 2 cups water
20ml/4 tsp leaf tea, preferably
   Darjeeling
5–6 green cardamom pods, bruised
1 cinnamon stick
4 cloves
2.5cm/1in piece fresh root
   ginger, peeled
300ml/10fl oz/1¼ cups milk
clear honey, to taste

Makes 3–4 glasses

MINT TEA
For a perfect after-meal drink, to help digestion, put a small bunch of mint leaves in a teapot and crush lightly. Add 10ml/2 tsp Chinese green tea and 300ml/10fl oz/1¼ cups boiling water. Stand for a minute and serve sweetened with honey, if you wish.

NUTRITIONAL INFORMATION Energy 35kcal/146kJ; Protein 2.5g; Carbohydrate 3.7g, of which sugars 3.7g; Fat 1.2g, of which saturates 0.8g; Cholesterol 5mg; Calcium 83mg; Fibre 0g; Sodium 38mg

1 Put the water, tea and spices into a pan and bring to the boil. Reduce the heat to low and simmer for 6–8 minutes.

2 Add the milk and increase the heat slightly. Simmer, uncovered, for 5–6 minutes until the tea has turned a pinkish-brown colour. Add more milk to taste. Remove from the heat and strain into individual cups. Add honey to taste and serve.

VARIATION
Use soya milk for its probiotic properties if you prefer, but instead of adding to the water before infusing, stir it in at the end and heat through without boiling.

INDEX